THRILLER

THRILLER

THE MUSICAL LIFE OF
MICHAEL
JACKSON

NELSON GEORGE

Da Capo Press
A Member of the Perseus Books Group

Editorial production by *Marra*thon Production Services, www.marrathon.net

DESIGN BY JANE RAESE
Set in 11.5-point New Caledonia

Cataloging-in-Publication Data for this book is available from the Library of Congress.

First Da Capo Press edition 2010
ISBN 978-0-306-81878-3

Published by Da Capo Press
A Member of the Perseus Books Group
www.dacapopress.com

Da Capo Press books are available at special discounts for bulk purchases in the U.S.
by corporations, institutions, and other organizations. For more information,
please contact the Special Markets Department at the Perseus Books Group,
2300 Chestnut Street, Suite 200, Philadelphia, PA 19103, or call (800) 810-4145,
ext. 5000, or e-mail special.markets@perseusbooks.com.

2 4 6 8 10 9 7 5 3 1

DEDICATED TO

MY EDITORS AND COWORKERS

AT *BILLBOARD* MAGAZINE

1982 TO 1989

CONTENTS

Startin' Somethin': An Introduction   1

PART ONE

2009   7

Going Back to Gary   15

The Voice   27

Audio/Visual I   41

New York, New York   49

Audio/Visual II   57

Black Hollywood   65

PART TWO

Thriller   75

"Wanna Be Startin' Somethin'"   87

CONTENTS

"Baby Be Mine"   95

"The Girl Is Mine"   101

"Thriller"   107

"Beat It"   113

"Billie Jean"   125

"Human Nature"   129

"PYT (Pretty Young Thing)"   133

"Lady in My Life"   139

PART THREE

Covering *Thriller*   145

The Fire, the Tour   161

The *Bad* Years   177

The Third and Final Father   187

Searching for Transcendence   205

This Is It   209

Epilogue   215

Acknowledgments   217

Index   219

About the Author   241

THRILLER

STARTIN' SOMETHIN'
AN INTRODUCTION

T IS 1971. I AM FOURTEEN YEARS OLD, AND I AM lacing up my black platform shoes. My mother is putting on her lipstick, and my sister, three years younger than I and a Jackson 5 fanatic, is picking out her Afro. As I wait on the ladies in my life, I sit on my bed in the public housing bedroom I share with my sister, flipping through copies of *Right On!* magazine, which, in the years before BET's *106 & Park,* is the way young black kids kept up with their teen idols. I read about a pickup basketball game at the Jackson family's Encino home and wonder if I could take Jermaine off the dribble.

My sister and mother are now ready. We grab our coats and then knock on our neighbors' door. Betty and her son exit their apartment, and we all ride down the elevator from the sixth floor. We live in the Samuel J. Tilden housing projects in Brownsville, Brooklyn, an area that is one of the worst ghettos in America.

We walk down Livonia Avenue, with the sixteen-story Tilden buildings to our right and the elevated IRT subway tracks looming to our left. Before we go upstairs to the elevated train, my mother buys Wrigley's Spearmint gum at the local candy store on Rockaway Avenue, as we all keep an eye out for the junkies who hang menacingly on the corner.

The long ride takes my family and friends from Brownsville, near the end of the IRT line, across Brooklyn through Crown Heights, Bedford-Stuyvesant, Park Slope, downtown Brooklyn, and then into Manhattan, running under Wall Street, through Greenwich Village up to the garment district, and finally to West 34th Street. On that long ride we talk about previous trips to Manhattan. My mother, who's studying to become a teacher, has taken us to many events in "the city," from *Mary Poppins* at Radio City Music Hall to Ossie Davis's *Purlie Victorious,* with Melba Moore, on Broadway.

But this family outing will be one of the most memorable of our lives. We get off at 34th Street and Seventh Avenue, joining the throngs of black and white families filing into Madison Square Garden. This version of the "World's Greatest Arena" is only about four years old and has already been the site of the first Ali-Frazier heavyweight championship fight and the New York Knicks' first NBA title. I've listened to so many games on the radio being played in this building, and yet it's only my second time inside.

We sit up high in the green seats to the right of the stage, but we are too excited to be upset about our nosebleed location. My mother is happy because Chuck Jackson, a deep-voiced soul singer and a longtime favorite, is one of the opening acts, obviously placed on the bill as an acknowledgment to all the parents in the house. (I don't realize until a few years later that the Commodores with Lionel Ritchie were the other opener; they performed a brief set.)

When the Jackson 5 takes the stage, the piercing screams of teenage girls fill the Garden. Michael moves swiftly across the stage, a little dynamo who reminds me of Mighty Mouse, the hyperactive Saturday morning cartoon character I love. The Jackson boys in their multicolored outfits glide across the Garden stage, and their Afros, perfect ovals of jet-black hair, look like halos. Though the crowd is very integrated, there's a palpable sense of pride emanating from the many black families in attendance.

The Jackson brothers, as well as their parents, Joe and Katherine, represent our potential and dreams. If they could emerge from the working-class slum of Gary, Indiana, so might my family escape public housing in Brooklyn. The Jacksons represent a growing sense of possibility for my family and me. Maybe one day I could even write a book about Michael Jackson. In a world where a black family, lead by an astoundingly talented little boy, could sell out an arena in New York City, anything could happen.

PART 1

2009

I WAS TAKING MY SEAT AT A PANEL DISCUSSION AT Brooklyn's Long Island University to celebrate the twentieth anniversary of Spike Lee's landmark film *Do the Right Thing* when I received a text from "Fab Five" Freddy Braithwaite, a friend and former host of *Yo! MTV Raps.* TMZ.com was reporting that Michael Jackson was dead. As the news filtered through the crowded lecture hall, folks were commenting on the irony of talking about an iconic 1980s film on the day that decade's most important pop star died.

But the connection among Spike, Michael, and me was more intimate than most folks at the event knew. In January 1984, on the night that Jackson was honored by the Guinness Book of World Records at the American Museum of Natural History, Dell published my first book, *The Michael Jackson Story,* a pocket-sized quickie biography of the singer. It would go on to sell more than 1 million copies and reach number three on the *New York Times* paperback best-seller list. I was twenty-six years old, and because of that book, for the first time in my young life I had something that could be described as disposable income.

With the money I made from the Michael Jackson book, I was able to afford my first apartment without a roommate. It was in a beautiful but then-unfashionable, brownstone-filled section of downtown Brooklyn called Fort Greene. There I befriended a young filmmaker named Spike Lee and saw an early cut of his film *She's Gotta Have It.* Over the course of 1985 I would invest $3,500 in Spike's film, a cinematic event that not only began his historic career, but also heralded a black film movement that still has impact today.

If I hadn't written that book, I would have never moved to Fort Greene or invested in Spike's work. My life, and to some small degree, black pop culture would have been different without my book and, far more significantly, without Michael's ascension to megastardom.

After the panel, I turned on my Blackberry® and found it filled with messages from friends and a slew of interview requests from publications, television shows, and radio broadcasts. LIU is a short walk from my apartment, so I went home, warmed up some leftovers, and sat quietly most of that evening, not returning messages or following the news.

At that moment, I didn't want to mourn in public. Nor did I want to speak to any aspects of Michael's life I didn't know anything about. I hate that cable news has become a place of empty speculation where supposed experts—many only with expertise in their own opinions—clutter the twenty-four-hour news cycle with hot air. My feelings were complicated by the fact that I had just signed a deal to write a book (this book) about the enduring influence of *Thriller* as a recording and cultural artifact. In anticipation of this work, I'd already looked into buying tickets for one of Michael's fifty shows at London's O_2 arena. In the immediate aftermath of his passing, I wrote a eulogy and posted it on my web site and did a few interviews, focusing on music and trying not to engage in the tabloid narrative of his death.

That night I thought about the great American cinema masterpiece *Citizen Kane,* Orson Welles's epic vision of the rich, brilliant, and ultimately doomed Charles Foster Kane, who died disgraced, alone, and unloved in his California mansion, far removed from the glory years of his media empire. The parallel to Jackson's life wasn't seamless, of course. Whereas Kane left this world at Xanadu, his own personal fantasyland of secret rooms, art, and creatures collected from around the globe, Michael's home, Neverland, had been taken from him by debtors. Instead, he died in a rented house under the care of a sketchy doctor who has been charged with manslaughter. In some ways, the better parallel was the director/actor Orson Welles himself, who was hailed as a genius in his twenties, declared a has-been in his thirties, and resurrected as a figure of camp appeal in the last decades of his life. With *Citizen Kane,* the young Welles created a masterpiece that haunted him for the rest of his life. *Thriller* played a similar role in Michael's life, attaining a level of international success he'd spend the last twenty-five years of his life trying to duplicate.

I'm a year older than Michael Jackson. I'm from a black working-class family and share with him the same astrological sign, none of which, rationally speaking, means a whole lot. What these parallels do suggest is that I was born at the right time to be swept up in the original burst of Jackson-mania and that, for much of my life, I could identify with him.

When I was a young writer, Michael was one of my primary subjects. Writing about him, I was able to get my first book deal. Not only did this help me financially, but it also inspired a couple of my best pieces of music criticism. His titanic success set many ships on fruitful journeys, and mine was just one of them. Now, as a middle-aged African American man, I marvel at his long, historic, singular career.

In 1999 ESPN asked me to contribute an essay on Michael Jordan to the book *Sports Century,* a look back at the greatest athletic achievements of the twentieth century. It was to be the book's last major essay, because it looked at the 1990s with Jordan as the decade's most significant player. I began that essay this way:

To write about Michael Jordan is to stand upon a mountain of press clips and pretend they don't exist. At the end of a century that made sports a global, 24 hour, over analyzed, zealously professional, obsessively marketed, and extravagantly played commodity, Jordan's career is the culmination of a long journey. Which means his every eye lash flutter has been photographed, catalogued, annotated, footnoted, and e-mailed by somebody at some time. So I will not be so foolish as to attempt to topple or even torch that mountain. It's too large for me to push and I lack the fuel to incinerate it completely.

I ended by observing that my essay would be laid "atop the mountain as it awaits some yet unseen 21st century bonfire."

By substituting Michael Jackson for Michael Jordan and substituting "entertainment business" for "sport," I could write the same paragraph. However hard it was for me to find something fresh to say about the basketball great, trying to do that with Jackson is even more challenging. The work I was commissioned to write was one of those "making of" a great LP volumes that have become popular in the postvinyl era.

With Michael's death, I felt a need to widen the scope of this book and be more comprehensive than I had originally intended. But I wouldn't change my focus. This is a book in which the music is central. It is the reason Michael Jackson matters. It is the reason he's a celebrity. It is why his personal life and tragic death are a matter of public record. So my perspective on Michael Jackson is in large part shaped by our respective life journeys from the 1950s into the twenty-first century.

But there is another view of Jackson that I want to honor as well. In the fall of 2009, I was talking with choreographer

Fatima Robinson on the set of VH1's *Hip Hop Honors,* an annual broadcast we'd both worked on for six years. Even in the middle of all the hip-hop acts we were working with, Michael Jackson's name came up. Fatima, one of the most creative and loved choreographers in pop music, had fond memories of working with Michael on his *Remember the Time* music video, and she shared a few with me.

But what I remember most about our conversation is that her nine-year-old son, Zuri, wanted a jheri curl, a hairstyle I thought had died back in the dark days of the twentieth century. Why would a lovely little black boy want one now? It turns out that since the entertainer's death, Zuri had become obsessed with Jackson, particularly the wet look of the *Thriller* era. The desire to emulate Jackson was cute, but Zuri also made an acute observation to go along with it, which was that he thought that there must have been two Michael Jacksons, one black, one white, and Zuri, himself dark brown, loved them both.

Growing up in Brownsville, I knew Michael only as a black child and later was disturbed by his transformations. For Zuri, and many children his age, Michael's racial identity is fluid, shifting from photo to photo, from old *Ed Sullivan Show* clips to the music video for "Liberian Girl." Zuri's easy acceptance of Jackson's multiple faces, unburdened by America's nasty racial history, is worth keeping in mind when we consider the music and life of this cultural icon.

Context changes meaning, sometimes elevating certain elements of a tale and, just as often, rendering others moot.

My Michael Jackson and Zuri's Michael Jackson are the same person, as his talent and DNA testify, but what "Michael Jackson" means can be as fluid as the dance moves he made famous. Despite the legal claims of his estate, the fanatical devotion of his most fervent fans, and those who think race doesn't matter (and others who know it does), the "meaning" of Michael Jackson isn't owned by anyone.

Michael Jackson's life raises so many questions—about Michael and about us. How do we collectively balance his musical/performing brilliance with his inappropriate relations with a litany of young boys? What do we make of his relationship to the black culture that nurtured him? Are there any lessons left from the success of *Thriller* that can be applied to the profoundly altered pop culture universe of the twenty-first century?

Here's what I know going in. *Thriller* was a product of the old record business model. It is a testament to the primacy of image over sound. It transcends racial lines by deliberately blurring those lines. It is about a determined pursuit of greatness and the difficulties that follow once greatness has been achieved. This is not a biography. It's a blend of musical criticism, memoir, and cultural history. My goal is to honor Michael Jackson's talent, while not overlooking his faults.

I hope this book will be of some use to Zuri one day, when he's older and looking for a text (that he will probably read on some kind of mobile device) that neither trivializes nor sensationalizes an artist he loved.

GOING BACK
TO GARY

F YOU DROVE DOWN FROM CHICAGO TO GARY, Indiana, at night back in the early 1960s, when the city's industrial engine was still roaring at full steam, you'd have seen flames rising up from steelmaking factories, a fiery symbol of economic vitality, ample employment opportunities, and unimpeded pollution. Gary was, in that respect, just one of the many tough Midwestern towns whose Rust Belt industries provided stability for residents and sturdy homegrown products for the nation.

For black America, Gary was a center of great racial pride, a place where our people were enjoying some of the fruits of postsegregation America. Richard Hatcher was elected mayor in 1967, making him one of the first African Americans to run a large city, a harbinger of a wave of black power grabs in cities around the nation. A few years after Hatcher's election, a national black political convention was held in Gary that briefly brought together all the disparate people and groups fighting for black empowerment.

But Hatcher's triumph was something of a Pyrrhic victory, made possible in part by the white flight that sent the ethnic working class to Indiana suburbs, in the process robbing Gary of essential tax dollars and encouraging state policymakers to turn their backs on the city. In a state with a history of massive Ku Klux Klan activity, not to mention actual Klan political power, dating back to the 1920s, Gary became Indiana's symbol of black folks gone wild. In response, the state cut back funding to the city and fearmongers got to work, both activities undermining Hatcher's authority.

In that respect Gary, Indiana, was no different from Newark, New Jersey, or Cleveland, Ohio, or Detroit, Michigan, newly chocolate cities that were systematically stripped of resources by state governments and banks' redlining. The urban riots of the 1960s, along with the spread of heroin throughout urban America, would eventually transform places like Gary from working-class ghettos into barely functional slums. But in the 1960s, the hopelessness that characterizes the twenty-first-century 'hood was not a given. People still believed that by legally pulling themselves up by the bootstraps, they could, if not clean up the ghetto, at least drag themselves free of its downward tug.

It is in this context that Joseph Jackson and Katherine Corse, married in 1949, birthed, raised, and developed one of the most successful families of entertainers in U.S. history. He was twenty-one and she was eighteen when they settled on the appropriately named Jackson Street. The young couple had nine kids, a brood that would have been perfect for a family of southern sharecroppers, but in a big city were a lot of mouths to feed. In two very crowded rooms Maureen (aka Reebee), Sigmond Esco (aka Jackie), Toriano Adoyl (aka Tito), LaToya, Marlon, Jermaine, Michael Joe, Steven Randell (aka Randy), and Janet lived under the guidance of Katherine and Joe.

Katherine did some part-time work at a Sears and at other local retailers, but she spent the majority of her time (and patience) providing a calming, constant, and spiritual presence for her family. She'd been struck by polio as a child, so she walked with a slight limp. Early on in the marriage, Katherine came under the influence of the Jehovah's Witnesses and was a regular at the local Kingdom Hall, along with her girls and young Michael, who of all her children would be the most interested in the Witnesses. Neither Joe nor the other sons seemed to have given the Witnesses more than token attention. Aside from going door to door hawking *The Watchtower* and *Awake* magazines around Gary in religious service, Katherine and her kids read the Witnesses' New World Translation of the Holy Scriptures, the belief's central text.

The Witnesses prophesize that humans are living in the last days of the present world order and that after Armageddon Christ will return to rule an earthly paradise populated by living Witnesses and 144,000 resurrected individuals. The idea of heavenly reward isn't as central to the Witnesses' doctrine as the idea of an earth repopulated by the righteous. Over the years some of this ideology would appear in Michael's lyrics and videos, refracted through his prism of pop culture.

JOE WAS REARED IN TENNESSEE by a stern, religious father, and as soon as he was old enough, Joe escaped to a big city in search of better-paying work and a more exciting life. Being a crane operator at U.S. Steel in the 1960s was a good job for any man with a high school education, much less a black man with ten mouths to feed. But Joe was filled with musical ambition and the restlessness that nearby opportunity creates. Why did he have to settle for a nine to five routine when a life of well-made suits, nightlife, and celebrity was just a well-played guitar solo away? In 1960s black America, there were many like Joe, black men of great ambition who knew that doors of opportunity were opening but were not quite sure where to find their personal keys. Like Walter Lee Younger in Lorraine Hansberry's classic 1959 play, *A Raisin in the Sun,* which is set just up the road from Gary on Chicago's South Side, Joe burned to be somebody.

Initially, Joe sought success through his own musical talent, playing guitar with a bluesy local bar band called the Falcons along with his brother Luther. (The Falcons were just one of numerous R&B groups named after birds. A more famous version of the Falcons would feature a young soul shouter named Wilson Pickett.) No recordings of Joe's band exist, but it's easy to imagine Joe pulling off his work clothes, washing up, putting on his flashiest suit, and then, guitar in hand, hitting a Gary nightspot named the Spot Lit or the Dew Drop Inn or one of those other puny Negro nightspots that dotted our big cities. It was an escape from the steel mill, the money worries, and the responsibilities of family life. Having kids—a joy. Feeding kids—a struggle. Making music—a pleasure.

But neither the Falcons as a group nor Joe as a musician proved very distinguished. The guitar sat in the Jackson house when Joe was out, not to be touched, but in a house full of kids it was as tempting as neglected birthday cake. That guitar was the centerpiece of sing-a-longs where the kids harmonized with Mom and Dad, singing spirituals and country and western tunes. It was the beginning of the Jackson family's musical journey and a traditional American family activity that was later mostly lost, first to TV and then to the Internet and text messaging.

When Joe was at work, the oldest boys soon began messing around with Joe's guitar, singing along to the R&B songs on Gary's soul station. The oft-told tale is that Tito, the steady, solid Jackson son who looks the most like his father, was caught with the instrument—the embodiment of the old man's unfulfilled dreams—and was challenged by Joe to show what he could do with it.

Impressed with Tito's musicianship, as well as that of Jermaine and Jackie, and with the support of Katherine, Joe's personal dream was replaced by a family quest. At the time, Joe didn't have to look far for a creative inspiration for an all-family R&B group. Just up North from Gary, in Chicago, was the Five Stairsteps.

Labeled "the first family of soul" well before the Jacksons, the Stairsteps were initially five of the six kids of Betty and Clarence Burke. When Joe was just starting to rehearse his sons in Gary, the Burkes were already playing on the amateur night circuit. Clarence, a detective with the Chicago Police Department, played bass and wrote songs, getting more involved on a creative level with his family act than Joe apparently ever did. The Five Stairsteps received their first recording contract after winning the amateur night contest at the South Side's Regal Theater one evening in 1965. Lead singer Clarence Junior, James, Dennis, thirteen-year-old Kenneth (known as Keni), and sister Alohe would initially record under the stewardship of Chicago soul star Curtis Mayfield. A couple of years later, to heighten the cuteness factor, three-year-old Cubie was added to the group.

But it wasn't until spring 1970, when the Jackson 5 was in the middle of a streak of number one hits, that the Five Stairsteps released its defining single. "O-o-h Child," a yearning ballad about two lovers trying to keep faith in each other and their future, was an instant classic, one still a staple on black oldies radio and used quite effectively in 1991's *Boyz n the Hood* to communicate a sense of innocence lost.

In the aftermath of Michael's death, Joe has been treated as the villain of the story, the Ike Turner of parenting: an overbearing mid-twentieth-century black man of little means who used and abused a gifted young artist, imposing psychological damage while making millions from his son's talent. If I challenge none of these assumptions and accept them unequivocally, not invoking the complexities of the individuals involved, I still see Joe Jackson as an undeniable, yet unlikeable hero. It was Joe who organized the musical interest of his sons into a polished act. It was Joe who drove the boys on long car rides to Chicago's Regal and New York's Apollo, who drilled dance routines with them in the backyard, who taught them to play instruments, and who gave them their first harmony lessons. And it was Joe who instilled in Michael the work ethic noticed by everyone who came in contact with him at Motown and in his adult career.

During the crucial adolescent and teenage years of the Jackson sons, when temptation and distraction, particularly drugs and alcohol, were everywhere, all of them stayed on the path. Not one of Joe's show biz kids became a tragedy like Frankie Lymon, at thirteen a singing/songwriting sensation from Spanish Harlem who, with his pals/backup group, the Teenagers, recorded the classic "Why Do Fools Fall in Love?" in 1956, displaying a crystal clear soprano voice and oodles of stage presence. By eighteen Lymon was a washed-up heroin addict, and by twenty-six he was dead, a victim of drugs, poor parental supervision, and a slew of bad marriages. The tale of Lymon, a briefly shining star now lost to obscurity, is way more typical in the history of black music than is the success story of the Jacksons.

Joe operated from enlightened self-interest, that sweet spot where what was good for him was equally good for everyone else. He drove, cajoled, and punched his children toward a goal that was, in 1968 Gary, Indiana, as unlikely as the idea of a black president. That two of his nine children became international superstars is nearly unprecedented in the history of pop.

Here is a hypothetical scenario. What if Joe heard Tito on guitar that day on Jackson Street and then listened to Tito, Jackie, and Jermaine sing and decided that they sounded "okay," but that he didn't have the inclination to support their musical ambitions? He had a full-time job already. He didn't need to be wrangling these kids in his free time. Without his tireless (or, in the minds of critics, demonic) rehearsals, the three oldest Jackson boys would have probably played some local talent shows and maybe some midwestern bars. Based on what we know of their talent, they might have scored a small record deal, but they might not have.

If Joe hadn't gotten behind making music as a way for his family to get out of Gary, the kids' work prospects would not have been great. To get his six boys to manhood in that town without any of them having a serious run-in with the law, or falling victim to the drugs rampant on those streets, would have been an amazing accomplishment in itself. Outside of the fading steel industry, there was little meaningful employment in the Gary of the 1970s and 1980s, so the older boys, their musical dreams behind them (but perhaps still dancing in their heads), would probably have headed to Chicago or out West in search of work and a fresh start. That unified Jackson family my African American peers and I so envied would have been fragmented by economic necessity.

MICHAEL, WHOSE PRECOCIOUS TALENT was evident to Katherine long before Joe paid attention, wouldn't have had the platform he needed without Joe's stewardship of his older brothers. Bright kid that he was, Michael would have read more books, watched more movies, and taken vocal lessons throughout his adolescence in Gary. Under any normal scenario, Michael would have watched his brothers' failures, would have studied the record business from a distance, and at some point between eighteen and twenty-two might have gone to a local college, maybe with a scholarship in literature or even dance. Or with the desire to perform burning in him, Michael could have headed to New York or Los Angeles in pursuit of a singing career.

By then, in the mid- to late 1970s, when the corporate takeover of black music had taken hold, his best chance at stardom would have been to bring his demo to one of the big boys (CBS, Warner Bros., RCA, Mercury) or one of the smaller, black-oriented labels they distributed. Because of Michael's great voice and charisma, he certainly would have attracted some attention, but would he have gotten a record deal? Let's say he did; he got a good deal at a big label committed to artist development and not a twelve-inch single deal for a disco record.

Without the early start his father's support provided, which led to him seeing the stars of 1960s soul up close and personal and to Motown signing the Jackson 5 to a record deal, Michael in the 1970s would have been a gifted but green young singer from the sticks. Maybe he would have had a career, but would he have become a global brand loved on every continent? I don't think so.

I write this not to absolve Joe of any real sins but to put his parenting skills in context. For me, Joe's attributes and faults were not untypical of many black fathers of his generation. Although Barack Obama and Bill Cosby are contemporary reigning symbols of black, white-collar fatherhood, working-class dads were the norm in black America for most of the twentieth century. They were men like my uncles and cousins who worked in the shipyards of Newport News, Virginia, and the fathers of the girls I dated in New York who drove city buses, emptied garbage cans, or worked construction to buy homes in Hollis, Queens, or Hempstead, Long Island. A lot of the fathers I encountered were inflexible authoritarians and ran their households as dictatorships, where their word was law, their wives were often silent partners, and any sign of insurrection was put down with force.

The racial history that nurtured this attitude is obvious to me, but still necessary to stress: Born pre–civil rights movement and raised in a dangerously segregated America, often toiling in a castrating environment at work, these Negro men viewed their homes as more than castles. They were places where the fathers' suppressed anger and resentment at white racism were understood and could be expressed. In their houses they were the boss. Within those walls they craved a respect that often no amount of wifely devotion or children's love could truly satisfy.

Stern, remote, definitely abusive, Joe has been portrayed as a cardboard villain in various books and even in the Motown-sanctioned TV movie of the band's rise. But Joe and his actions make no sense without this black working-class context.

During my nine years as a music trade reporter, I had many encounters with Joe, both on the phone and at his Los Angeles office (which was located in the same Sunset Boulevard building as Motown). To say Joe was a pleasant, warmhearted man would be a lie. He was anxious, rather prickly, and, when he focused his lionlike features my way, definitely intimidating. His infamous appearance outside the BET Awards with CNN just after his son's death did him no favors.

"My father was real strict with us—real strict," Michael wrote in *Moon Walk,* his clearly ghostwritten but still useful 1988 biography edited by Jacqueline Kennedy Onassis. "I'd get beaten for things that happened mostly outside rehearsal. Dad would make me so mad and hurt that I'd try to get back at him and get beaten all the more. I'd take a shoe and throw it at him or I'd just fight back, swinging my fists. . . . I would fight back and my father would kill me, just tear me up. . . .We had a turbulent relationship."

Joe Jackson was Michael's biological father and the first of several artistic mentors. It was Joe who gave his son his first showcase and structure, molding and scarring him in equal measure.

THE VOICE

ICHAEL'S LONG RECORDING CAREER AFFORDS us a unique opportunity to listen to a beautiful human voice as it evolves from childhood to middle age. There are gospel recordings of Aretha Franklin at twelve from a Detroit church. There are homemade childhood tapes scattered around from artists as diverse as Kurt Cobain and Beyoncé. But Michael was recorded professionally from age eight to fifty, enabling us to hear a great vocal artist refine his craft, using new technology and his evolving understanding of vocal technique, and adapting to the changes wrought by age.

That's why it's fascinating to listen to the pre-Motown records the Jackson 5 made in 1966 for the little Gary, Indiana–based Steeltown Records. Steeltown was owned by Gordon Keith, a local steelworker Michael always called Mr. Keith. The band on these recordings is decidedly loose.

Apparently, the rhythm section was the Jackson 5 paired with older horn players and backing vocalists. Compared to the crispness of Motown or Stax records circa 1968, which were as tight as a sailor's knot, the four sides of the early Jackson 5 are not exciting and are certainly not well played.

MICHAEL'S LEAD VOCAL ON "BIG BOY" is his most engaging of these early performances. The lyric is the tale of a young boy asserting his maturity to a skeptical woman, and Michael's vocal approach is more adult than in his early Motown recordings. "Big Boy" is a very traditional sounding soul record, and the eight-year-old singer is mimicking older singers such as Ronnie Isley or Marvin Gaye, while playing down his natural kiddie exuberance. The talent is there but not the excitement that would soon become his trademark, because on this record a boy is imitating a man, a ploy designed to charm Negro adults. This kind of imitation was quite popular at house parties of my childhood. The opening skit of Eddie Murphy's Robert Townsend–directed *Raw* concert film is a bit with a young Murphy entertaining a room of his parents' friends. I was known for my Jackie Wilson split, the singer's signature dance move, where the ex–Golden Glove boxer would slide his legs out to the sides while his torso dropped to the floor. When I did this right, I could usually stay up a little later, sneak a shot of rum and coke, and maybe get a quarter from an impressed houseguest. Other kids I knew could shimmy and shake like James Brown or imitate the Temptations' choreography.

Such parodies by kids of adult entertainers were staples of amateur nights all over the country. So in that respect neither the Jackson 5's stage show nor Michael's attempted vocal ventriloquism was remarkable at the time. What the Jacksons needed, and what Steeltown couldn't deliver, was a vision of what could be instead of a rehash of soul clichés. With a singer as young as Michael (or Jermaine for that matter), the challenge was not to give the audience what it already had, but to find a youthful approach that, yes, exploited the singer's age while continuing to entertain adults. What these records lacked, technical limitations aside, was a point of view.

Now point of view was what Motown specialized in. It crafted songs to define a singer's persona as well as, and usually better than, any musical institution in history. In fact, the struggle within the company over that point of view defined the Jackson 5's first two years with Motown. The Motowner who first found and believed in Joe Jackson's boys was a B list singer-bandleader named Bobby Taylor, who, with his band, the Vancouvers (one of the more curious names for an R&B aggregation ever), had performed on shows with the group a number of times on the chitlin' circuit.

The Vancouvers, an integrated band that included future stoner comedian Tommy Chong, had signed with Motown in 1966 and was considered a major vocal talent by many around the company, including Marvin Gaye. Bobby and the Vancouvers would have a hit in 1968 with "Does Your Mama Know About Me?" a song about an interracial love affair, very much in keeping with Taylor's countercultural credentials as a grad of UC-Berkeley.

Unfortunately, Bobby's attitude was, in a very 1960s way, not very respectful of authority, a trait that didn't take you far within the very bureaucratic Motown structure. So even though Bobby would not become a star himself, the man knew great talent when he heard it. "In the summer of 1968," he told writer David Ritz,

> we were playing the Regal on the same bill as Jerry Butler, the Chi-Lites, and Little Miss Soul. The Jackson 5 opened the show. They had won the amateur contest a number of times, which meant they were now playing for pay. Michael was at the height of his James Brown thing. I mean he had James Brown down—the spin, the moves, the mike action, the whole bit. It was weird and wonderful to see this little kid singing like a sexy man. Michael would do "Cold Sweat" and "I Got the Feeling" with feelings you can't fake. His brothers were steppin' behind him, and the whole thing was dynamite. I saw enough. I knew they were ripe, so I said to Joe "I'm taking y'all to Detroit."

At his own expense Bobby brought the boys and Joe to Detroit in the summer of 1968, a year after the riots that permanently scarred Motor City. He put them up at his place, where he worked with them on harmonies and enunciation. The leap from raw live performance to studio professionalism can be a big one, and Taylor, as much as anyone, provided Michael and his brothers with that initial education.

Joe had succeeded on the club level by cultivating Michael's natural soul-singing instincts. Eventually, Michael would add other singing styles to his bag of vocal tricks, but at the age of nine he was deep into the tradition, a gift that Taylor saw clearly. In recording the Jackson 5's initial Motown records, he "never thought about pop. Crossover was some marketing concept that didn't interest me at all. This boy, this little Michael Jackson, could blow. He had the goods. As a singer, he was so straight-ahead black that I knew he'd take his place alongside Ray Charles. In Michael, I had me a soul singer."

In the West Grand Boulevard studios, Taylor cut tracks with the Funk Brothers, superb Motown session musicians, but laid down only scratch vocals. With the Jacksons' return to school in Gary imminent, he didn't want to rush the real recording process. So the vocals that you hear on the Taylor-produced soul sessions, recordings that weren't widely available until a 1995 four-CD set, were primarily recorded in January and February 1970 after the Jacksons moved from Gary to Los Angeles.

But in these initial Los Angeles sessions, Taylor was very much in charge and took Michael and his brothers on a very soulful journey, cutting thirty-plus tracks with many of the session cats who would dominate the West Coast R&B scene in the 1970s: guitarist Wah Wah Watson, percussionist Eddie "Bongo" Brown, and Detroit refugees such as drummer Uriel Jones and guitarist Jack Ashford. A cover of the Isley Brothers' "It's Your Thing" features Michael hitting and stretching notes with a syncopation that matches the track's razor-sharp cymbal sound. Not surprisingly, a hip-hop–favored remix of this track, featuring Michael's vocals with contemporary instrumentation, is a club favorite today; his young voice sits as comfortably in the groove's pocket as it would on "Rock with You."

The Jackson 5 rendition of the Four Tops' "Reach Out I'll Be There," on which Michael shares vocals with Jermaine, is performed at a slower tempo than the original, and Michael's vocals are bluesier than Levi Stubbs's more operatic inter-pretation. The stunner of these tracks is a cover of Ray Charles's "A Fool for You." Charles wrote and recorded this early soul classic three years before Michael was born, yet Michael sings it with an emotional maturity that seems im-possible for someone who was eleven at the time. It's ab-solutely as good a Michael Jackson performance as any in his career.

Unfortunately for Taylor, Berry Gordy's commercial in-stincts allowed him to see behind the brilliance of one perfor-mance and take in the big picture. "BG [Berry Gordy] accused me of cutting tunes that were old fashioned," Taylor recalled. "But to me they were classics. I wanted to feed Michael's soul." Ultimately, Gordy removed Taylor as the Jackson 5's producer. Of the many tracks he produced with the group, a gorgeous cover of Smokey Robinson and the Miracles' "Who's Lovin' You," which is far superior to the original, was the only one to get noticed during the initial wave of Jackson-mania. It was the B side of "I Want You Back," the first of the Jackson 5's number one singles, and the contrast between the two performances reflected Gordy's amazing pop instincts and the versatility of tender young Michael's instrument. Whereas the folks at Steeltown, Joe, and Bobby Taylor had all seen Michael's voice as a vehicle for a kid to sing as an adult, Gordy saw that the real money was in having a kid with adult skills sing as a kid.

Replacing Taylor as the Jackson 5's in-studio point person was a very unlikely character named Deke Richards, a white guitarist/songwriter in his midtwenties and the son of a Hollywood screenwriter. He'd been seduced by Elvis Presley's "Heartbreak Hotel" and picked up guitar soon after. At fourteen he wrote a song with the prophetic title "Bubblegum." The teenage Richards formed his own band, Deke and the Deacons, which played R&B hits in Los Angeles and around the valley. The group broke up in 1965, and the twenty-one-year old musician wound up backing a white female singer named Debbie Dean. She'd been the first white artist signed to Motown back in 1961, and despite minimal sales success, she had remained in the Motown orbit.

Dean hustled up a meeting with Gordy at the Century Plaza Hotel with Richards in tow. The mogul liked what he heard and took them on as a songwriting team. Over the next few years, as Gordy spent increasing amounts of time in LA,

Richards's songwriting skills and amiable demeanor landed him in Gordy's good graces.

In 1968 Richards proved to be the right man in the right place. The legendary H-D-H team (Brian Holland, Lamont Dozier, Eddie Holland) that had crafted huge pop hits for the Supremes and the Four Tops, and who would have been naturals to mentor the Jackson 5, sued the company for back royalties and left to start a label. Initially, Gordy organized an ad hoc team of writer-producers to keep the Supremes hits coming. Along with Richards, LA-based Frank Wilson and Motown vets Pam Sawyer, R. Dean Taylor, and Hank Cosby (who'd done a lot of work with Stevie Wonder) were brought together at Detroit's Pontchartrain Hotel to craft some post–H-D-H material. Out of this loose ensemble, dubbed the Clan, came "Love Child," the tale of an inner-city girl and the pressures in her life, which was unusually realistic for Motown. But the Clan was a stopgap measure, not a long-term solution. Lacking cohesion and any loyalty to each other, the Clan dissolved in disputes over credits and royalties.

In the aftermath, Richards went back to LA still excited about the idea of collaborative songwriting and determined to build his own team. With Gordy's blessing, Richards recruited two gifted college-trained musicians, keyboardists Freddie Perrin and Fonce Mizell. Because Perrin and Mizell were already friends and used to collaborating, they were open to giving the team concept a try.

Initially, the trio was working with Gladys Knight and the Pips and came up with a track called "I Want to Be Free." How this song evolved into "I Want You Back" is the subject of several slightly different stories. Richards has told interviewers that when they played the tune for Gordy, he suggested they adapt it for "the boys" by giving it a Frankie Lymon feel, making the lyric about a guy who loses his girl.

Gordy has written that he had the hook "Oh baby, give me one more chance" in his head for weeks before passing it along to the young trio for further development, not mentioning the Knight connection. Either way, the Lymon reference is the real key, because the resulting lyric harks back to "Why Do Fools Fall in Love?" in that both records are simultaneously upbeat and plaintive, fun and vaguely melancholy, a balance that somehow has mass appeal. Years ago I wrote of "I Want You Back": "The resulting record was an explosive burst of youthful enthusiasm backed by immaculate, dynamic production and a clever lyric to which Berry had clearly contributed his expertise. Once again Berry had demonstrated his mastery of the increasingly anachronistic three minute single."

Poised at a moment when black music was about to expand its artistic boundaries, when singles would go from three minutes to four and five, when albums would replace singles as the creative and financial centerpiece of black pop music, the Jackson 5's breakthrough records were throwbacks to Motown's mid-1960s formula, this time infused with youthful vitality. These records were new and old at the same time, part throwbacks to the songs Gordy wrote for Jackie Wilson in the 1950s, yet deeply influenced by the late 1960s funky pop as played by Sly and the Family Stone.

With Berry Gordy on board as one-quarter of the entity known as the Corporation, the team spent $10,000 on the single, more than three times the cost of the average Motown recording in 1969. Much of that money was spent perfecting the vocals of Michael and his brothers. Unlike Taylor's more spontaneous sounding tracks, "I Want You Back," as well as "ABC," "The Love You Save," and the other early up-tempo Corporation productions, Michael's every line was scrutinized for pronunciation and phonetics. From wonderful ad-libs ("Just look over your shoulder honey") to the studied absence of the churchy moans that delighted Taylor, the records convey beautifully manufactured joy.

The three hits are sung fast and furious, as if a starter pistol has gone off with the first note and three minutes ahead is the finish line. Labeled "bubblegum soul" by fans and detractors alike, the term captures the essence of teen appeal soul, so full of craftsmanship and spirit that the tunes would become templates for groups from the Osmonds to New Edition to New Kids on the Block and many more.

Motown's production-line philosophy had always been that if a particular style worked, you keep recording in that style until consumer exhaustion set in. So subsequent Jackson 5 up-tempo tracks ("Goin' Back to Indiana," "Mama's Pearl," "Sugar Daddy") all contained strands of the DNA of

"Want" in rhythm arrangement, melody, and the Jackson 5's vocals. This lesson wouldn't be lost on young Michael, who saw that in repetition of vocal tics, attention to the meticulous details of tight harmony, and the stamina to manufacture emotion through numerous takes was the key to record sales.

The other crucial lesson Michael learned in the school of Motown, one that he'd employ often in his mature recordings a decade later, was the right vocal approach to a pop ballad. Unlike an R&B love song, wherein a singer has free reign to sing in and around the melody, a pop stylist works within the melody, only really cutting loose toward the last third of the song. Good lyrics help, but a memorable, well-structured melody with a tasty bridge allows a smart singer to elevate everything from a generic lyric to a plain old silly love song.

Michael's education in the pop ballad came not from the Corporation but from Hal Davis, who'd opened Motown's Los Angeles office and waited patiently for the company's operations to shift west. Eventually, Davis would become Motown's most reliable staff producer-writer of the 1970s, equally adept at pop songs and disco tracks. At the time, he was anxious to work with the Jackson boys, knowing that they were a priority for the company.

Instead of trying to compete with the Corporation with up-tempo tracks, Davis, along with several collaborators, including the very gifted Willie Hutch, went in a different direction. Davis, who in a few years would guide Diana Ross through the slow simmer and release of the epic "Love

Hangover," was a master of modulating and slowly intensify-ing a vocal performance. As a producer, the Jacksons de-scribed him as a stern taskmaster and a teacher; in Michael, he'd find an A-plus student.

Michael's vocal on "I'll Be There" is sweetly angelic, the voice of a choirboy. In a way, the song is a hymn. The lyric, credited to Hutch, Davis, Gordy, and arranger Bob West, is about reassurance in a time of trouble. The song calls for bringing "salvation back," an obvious religious reference. But the rest of the lyric is vague enough that it could be God speaking to his believers, a man singing to a woman, or, of course, a small boy talking to his parents.

With a touch of echo effect on his voice, Michael sounds like a ringing bell when balanced against Jermaine's midrange voice and choral backing vocals that sound like very soulful Catholic school boys. Michael colors within the lines of the melody until the ending's famously calculated ad-lib ("Just look over your shoulder honey"). This is a very sculptured performance, and it remains so resonant that in 2009, nearly three decades after the song's release, All-State insurance used an a cappella version, highlighting Michael's affecting schoolboy vocal in a series of TV commercials.

"I'll Be There" is the template for the piercingly emotive pop balladeer Michael would become. You can trace a direct line from this 1970 performance to "She's Out of My Life" to "Human Nature" to "You Are Not Alone," as impressive a catalog of controlled, melody-enhancing performances as ex-ists in American music.

THE VOICE

"Maybe Tomorrow" is my favorite Michael Jackson vocal of the early 1970s. Where "I'll Be There" is polished pop, "Maybe Tomorrow" is the kind of sweet soul record Thom Bell was making in Philadelphia with the Delfonics or Stylistics, with its brightly tuned guitars, agile strings, and piano-based hooks. The difference is that Bell's productions usually featured a falsetto lead. In contrast on "Maybe Tomorrow" Michael begins by singing the opening verses in his lower range at a slow pace, raising his voice briefly with the ascending melody, and then settling back down.

As the arrangement swells midway through, Michael rises up in his register again and never returns to that original approach. Instead, he sings higher and picks up his pace as tambourines, piano, and strings become more active. By the song's last third, Michael is loose, stretching out words, getting gospel gritty, and bouncing off Jermaine's more strained interjections.

"Maybe Tomorrow," a song of deep romantic yearning, was an instant ghetto classic, a record that sounded better to me at a red light project house party than on the radio, a record to slow dance to with the sexiest girl in the room. In the 1990s, rapper Ghostface Killah and producer Rza used it as the foundation for "All That I Got Is You," a tale of melancholy hopefulness that maintained the tone of the original while making it modern. Michael Jackson and Ghostface Killah—connected by sampling and yearning.

AUDIO/VISUAL 1

THE BLACK-AND-WHITE FILM SHOT IN DETROIT, Michigan, in 1968, recorded Michael Jackson, his four brothers, and their backup musicians performing in a rehearsal studio. Bobby Taylor, their first Motown mentor, organized the shoot to showcase his young discoveries for an absent Berry Gordy. It was Michael's de facto first music video.

No sequined glove. No lighting cues. No preening. No bombast. Just a surreal display of James Brown– and Jackie Wilson–styled singing and dancing by a pint-sized dynamo for whom visual presentation would be as important as audio.

Once signed to Motown and moved west, first to the Hollywood Hills and then to their own Encino compound, the Jacksons had their image expertly crafted by Motown executive Suzanne de Passe and other Motown staffers. Gordy would say: "We didn't have to make them into kids from down the street. They were those kids."

The Jackson kids were unusually well dressed. Their immaculately maintained Afros signaled black pride. The color and texture palate of their clothing was hip psychedelic (fringe jackets, suede vests, embroidered bell-bottoms), with a few streetwise touches, such as applejack caps.

As kids in Brooklyn, my friends and I kept up with the Jacksons' adventures and style via *Right On!* magazine. In the vast library of pop periodicals that have chronicled the life of Michael Jackson, there should be a special place of honor reserved for *Right On!* As the name suggests, *Right On!* was a product of the 1970s. It was not a black nationalist publication full of propaganda and pathos, but rather a pulpy pub that celebrated the newly emerging black teen pop culture. It was the *Tiger Beat* of the bushy Afro, bell-bottomed, body poppin', *Soul Train*–watching generation. The black teen as a particular consumer target market was a fresh idea in the post–civil rights era, an idea intimately tied to Motown's marketing of the Jackson 5.

With breathless, high-energy prose and colorful covers that promised exclusives, *Right On!* existed to provide adolescents like my sister and me with every officially sanctioned detail of the Jackson 5's life. This wasn't *Jet* or *Ebony*, written for and by righteous adults proud of every step of black progress. It was written for kids who'd experienced the civil rights struggle through television and newspaper headlines. We were gonna have more fun than our parents, and the J5, in multicolored gear, was a symbol of a more carefree vision of black life.

The Big Three networks' prime-time variety shows were still America's way of seeing new talent when the Jackson 5 debuted and the boys from Gary made the rounds. Ed Sullivan's introduction of them on one of his legendary CBS Sunday night broadcasts was so important to the Jackson family that snippets from it were used during the 1981 tour to introduce a Motown medley. *Soul Train,* Don Cornelius's syndicated dance show, a Saturday morning staple on stations around the nation, had the Jackson 5 and later the Jacksons on many times. You can watch the boys grow up via YouTube clips from all these shows.

I think the visual triumph of this period was the Saturday morning cartoon series that Motown sold to ABC. The twenty-three-show series ran from September 1971 to September 1973, and although it didn't feature the Jacksons' actual voices, it did use their photos in the opening credits and showcased two songs per episode. Berry Gordy, acting as their manager, catalyzed many stories in his efforts to publicize the group. When I think of this series, the word "normal" comes to mind. Having black kids (alongside Bill Cosby's *Fat Albert*) on television on Saturday mornings helped to make black people less exotic to white peers. The hijinks of the Jackson 5 were no different from those of *Josie and the Pussycats* or *Alvin and the Chipmunks.* The cartoons weren't profound, but they had an impact. The cartoons, just as much as the songs, helped invest my generation in

Michael, so that when he went solo, many white folks, as well as black, had spent part of their childhood connected to him.

MICHAEL APPEARED IN ONLY ONE Hollywood-financed movie during his fifty years—*The Wiz* in 1978 (unless we count the 1980s Disney theme park ride/video *Captain EO*). As a young wannabe African American actor in the 1970s and 1980s, Michael wasn't cast in more films for the same reasons his peers weren't—his skin color. In that era there was only one black movie star at a time: Sidney Poitier had given way to Richard Pryor, who gave way to Eddie Murphy. The absence of roles for brown young men like Michael Jackson wasn't unusual.

Over time, as Michael's looks evolved, either because of vitiligo, calculated skin lighting, and/or cosmetic surgery, it became increasingly hard to imagine Michael in very many roles despite his massive celebrity. If a Steven Spielberg mentioned a possible role for Michael, it was usually as a character in *Peter Pan* or some other piece that would place him outside workaday reality. He was a real person, yet no filmmaker could figure out how he'd play one on screen.

Michael's other hurdle was his speaking voice. Most critics and audiences vastly underrate tone of voice in the movie star's tool kit. A pleasing, rich voice that can convey a wide range of emotion is as essential on screen as big eyes or a strong chin. Michael's light, airy voice, much more the voice of a child than of a man, would seriously limit his acting choices. One of the ironies of Michael's career is that he had one of the greatest singing voices, capable of projecting complicated emotions, while his speaking voice made Hollywood view him (when it paid attention at all) as a perpetual adolescent. Yet despite Michael's rare acting jobs, from that first audition tape in Detroit to the posthumous *This Is It* concert film, few entertainers have had such a detailed record of their performance life captured on film, video, and, finally, high definition.

As an adult, Michael later created his own minimovies, and he rarely settled for mundane depictions. He possessed a heightened view of himself, by turns whimsical, tortured, and, toward the end, megalomaniacal. These projections of Michael as a visual icon were a more direct portal into his dreams than even his music was.

Most of his TV appearances in the early to mid-1970s extended the strategy that Joe had begun back in Gary, playing heavily on the juxtaposition of Michael's youth with his poise. Dressed in the layered gear that was hip circa the early 1970s, Michael's look was compatible with that of music icons such as Donny Hathaway and Curtis Mayfield. Though Michael was a child, his clothes said he was a peer of the R&B greats just as much as his voice did.

When Michael donned a tuxedo or some other outfit associated with mainstream show business, the effect was even more striking. There's a wonderful clip of Michael, dressed in a dark suit and fedora and with a coat slung over his shoulder, singing a parody of "It Was a Very Good Year" by a street lamp. Michael's Frank Sinatra–styled performance showed he was capable of mimicking all kinds of American stars, not just R&B idols.

In all of the performances during these years (*Soul Train, Ed Sullivan Show, Goin' Back to Indiana*), Michael's face was open and his delivery pure. Every word he sang was convincing (even when he might not have understood all the lyrics); the canned interview responses or the silly shirts he was dressed in did not diminish his accomplishment. As a child he was so eager to please, so sure that he could sell anything by committing to the material, that the often-corny vibe surrounding these performances had no effect on their power. He never gave a hint that he thought the material was beneath him (though he knew it was). If there was any arrogance in this young boy, it was in his unflinching belief that anything could be sold through the power of performance.

The most obvious example of this commitment was the twelve episodes of the Jackson family series that aired from June 16, 1976, to March 9, 1977. Michael, who celebrated his eighteenth birthday during the season, was saddled with carrying a show designed to sell the family as an act ready for a long, happy run at a Las Vegas casino/hotel. In 1974 the Jacksons had had a very successful stint in Vegas, setting box office records as they expanded the Jackson 5, bringing Randy, LaToya, and precocious Janet into the act. That venture had been Joe and Katherine's initiative, done without Motown's care and cooperation, a harbinger of the family's break from the label in 1975.

In a sense, the CBS show was an extension of Joe's original vision of the Jackson 5. He'd built an act that Motown took in, shined up, and developed. But now, away from Motown and totally under Joe's control again (with his management partner Richard Aarons), the act was a full-family spectacle.

Michael didn't like the show, and he was right to be unhappy. Despite his enthusiasm, and that of his siblings, the thirty-minute shows were painfully lame. Each show opened with an extended Vegas arrangement of a Jackson 5 or Jacksons hit. Midway through the song, the music dropped down and the brothers introduced themselves to the audience. Tito often made a labored joke about his brothers being his backup group. Then the Jackson Sisters (as they were billed) came out, and the opening song finished.

After a commercial break, Marty Cohen (the lackluster comedy team of Samuels and Cohen were series regulars) did a quick comic bit as a newsreader before the scene changed to a newsstand where the Jacksons were pouring through celebrity magazines to the consternation of the owner, played by Jim Samuels. A celebrity guest—Joey Bishop, McKenzie Phillips, Sonny Bono—joined the Jacksons to comment on the magazines' fabricated reports of their lives (shades of "Leave Me Alone"). This was usually followed by a dance/comedy number, such as the Jackson family in 1950s greaser gear singing "Do the Fonz."

The choice of guests on the show reflected CBS's nervousness about the appeal of a prime-time show starring eight black siblings. So *Tonight Show*/variety TV hacks such as Joey

Bishop, Tim Conway, Dom Deluise, and Sonny Bono were booked to reassure white viewers that nothing too radical (or racial) was going to happen in their living rooms. In twelve episodes, only three had black guests (Muhammad Ali, Tina Turner, Redd Foxx).

Other than being the lead singer of the group, Michael was unremarkable in the CBS show. He was one piece of a very mawkish package.

NEW YORK,
NEW YORK

THE FIRST REHEARSAL FOR THE MOVIE VERSION of the all-black musical *The Wiz* was in October 1977. This was his first work on a major creative project without his family's involvement and his first extended stay in the Big Apple (he was there on and off well into spring 1978). "During this period of my life, I was searching, both consciously and unconsciously," Michael would later write. "I was feeling some stress and anxiety about what I wanted to do with my life now that was I an adult. I was analyzing my options and preparing to make decisions that could have a lot of repercussions."

The Wiz marked Michael's first collaboration with Quincy Jones, who supervised the score to what was to become a big budget, ill-fated, and critically maligned project. Much was said later by both men about their first meeting on set when Quincy helped Michael correctly pronounce the name of the Greek philosopher Socrates. But aside from this relationship, another significant influence on Michael's musical and emotional development during this time was New York City itself.

The many months he spent acting in *The Wiz* placed him in the Big Apple at the height of the disco era, a time when black, white, gay, and Latin dance clubs filled my hometown. With Diana Ross, Liza Minnelli, or many of the incredible company of dancers who worked on *The Wiz,* Michael was a regular at Studio 54 (as journalist Anthony Haden Guest mentioned in his history of the club, *The Last Party*).

I was in college at the time *The Wiz* was shooting around town, and I was working as a writer for the black weekly the *Amsterdam News.* I'd hear regular reports, from girls clocking this very eligible bachelor's moves, of Michael being seen out at this or that club. He was staying on posh Sutton Place, an isolated street overlooking the East River and a short drive over the 59th Street Bridge to Kaufman Astoria Studios in Queens, where *The Wiz* was being shot. Sutton Place was also close to the Midtown hot spots he'd visit on days off.

Studio 54 was a study in hedonism, with bare-chested pretty-boy barbacks and willowy women in high platform shoes cruising the room, anxiously looking for drugs and sexual hookups. The upper balcony of the converted old vaudeville hall didn't have any seats, but it did have flat surfaces where all manner of sexual activity took place. This was also true of the unisex restrooms on the mezzanine.

Even though there is no record of Michael Jackson indulging in drugs or sex at Studio 54, he was definitely witness to New York disco culture at the height of its glittery glory. Living in New York during that period, no matter how long his workdays or how sheltered his suite, Michael could not have ignored the city's voracious nightlife as well as the stark contrast between poverty and the city's party life.

You can find pictures online of Michael, shirt open to mid-chest, Afro still intact, and shiny disco belt around his slim waist, snapping his fingers as three tall, tan, and terrific-looking black women in iridescent hot pants surround him—all four singing happily along to a song—maybe one of his. You'll see Michael was also photographed with Studio 54's crazed co-owner Steve Rubell and Aerosmith frontman Steven Tyler. You'll see Michael at the center of a posed photo, surrounded by the gay disco act the Village People and actresses Valerie Perrine and Jane Fonda. Among sexy women, campy gay singers, and rock stars, Michael lived the nightlife of a young celebrity, but without the sex and drugs so often associated with that scene.

At least that's the official story. Any youthful first-time sexual experiences during this period of Michael's life would probably have happened when he worked with hundreds of dancers on *The Wiz* set and hung out at NYC clubs. And when I say experimentation, I do not mean he had intercourse. A friend who socialized with Michael later in his life always thought of him as a voyeur of adult sexual play—that he'd watch people make out or go further, enjoy the spectacle, maybe giggle, but not participate, holding onto his Virgo sense of eternal innocence. Moving through Studio 54 or Elaine's or Leviticus or the Paradise Garage—legendary Uptown, black, and gay discos of the 1970s—he could easily have gotten a sexual education without taking off a stitch of clothing.

THE UNIQUE FUSION OF SOUND and sensibilities that was New York's soundtrack in the late 1970s was defined by radio station WBLS and its program director/superstar DJ, Frankie "Hollywood" Crocker. Deep voiced, ridiculously cool, and decidedly stylish, Crocker was also the Big Apple's leading black concert promoter, which meant he decided what got played on New York's number one music station and he profited when those same acts performed at one of the city's major concert venues. It gave Crocker incredible power in New York and in the industry.

Michael was very familiar with Crocker because he held sway over which of Michael's records got played in the nation's biggest record-buying market. Michael may have gone to Studio 54 when he was in town, but Crocker was one of the glam crowd folks who made it hot. Crocker, in fact, was a presence at every one of the city's important discos.

"Instead of waiting for the promotion men to come to him

to pitch records," wrote Peter Shapiro in *Turn the Beat Around: The Secret History of Disco,*

> Crocker went out on the disco circuit—frequenting places like the aspiration black disco Leviticus at 45 West 33rd Street, Studio 54 and, most famously, the Paradise Garage—to discover his own, and the playlist changed accordingly. Crocker's mix of music was elegant, suave, sophisticated and, most important, color-blind. Crocker played off the wall (for black radio) stuff like Led Zeppelin and Bob Dylan's "Gotta Serve Somebody" and long album cuts as well as singles.

I wasn't always a fan of Crocker's eclecticism given that he decided that the funkiest bands of the era (Cameo, Bar-Kays, Con Funk Shun) didn't blend well with his disco mix. Nevertheless, he opened up black audiences to Euro-disco, breaking Donna Summer's "Love to Love You Baby" and the wonderful alternative dance band Dr. Buzzard's Original Savannah Band, among many. Crocker's vision dominated New York in the late 1970s, and his slogan announced, "If I'm not on your radio, your radio isn't on." During the time Michael was shooting *The Wiz*, this was absolutely true.

OF COURSE, THE IMPACT OF DISCO was not confined to the New York hip; it was everywhere: in movie theaters and on uncool Top 40 AM stations. And in these venues, the Bee

Gees ruled. Once a Beatles-inspired harmony group, the brothers Gibb (Maurice, Robin, and Barry) had first been seduced by disco on their 1975 album, *Main Course,* produced by R&B veteran Arif Mardin. Buoyed by hits such as "Nights on Broadway," the Bee Gees went in a new direction, emphasizing falsettos in both backing and lead vocals. In 1978, the Gibb brothers contributed several new songs to the *Saturday Night Fever* soundtrack, which also contained dance gems by the Trammps ("Disco Inferno"), Tarvares ("More Than a Woman"), and KC and the Sunshine Band ("Boogie Shoes").

But it was "Stayin' Alive," in which an anxious New Yorker sings of big-city survival in high-pitched multipart harmony over a slinky, smooth beat, that dominated pop culture, while irritating lots of R&B professionals who felt that black groups were already making this kind of record and were being ignored. From a musical point of view, black music vets had a legit gripe. But as a pop cultural event, *Saturday Night Fever* transcended the boundaries of race. It was a true audio/visual event, a pop cultural explosion, ignited by John Travolta's scruffy charisma and dirty dancing elegance. His white suit and black shirt, beautifully framed by director John Badham's camera, added a visual dimension to the Bee Gees' music that the painfully uninteresting band could not. (The group's video for "Stayin' Alive," shot in a railyard, was so bad it was funny.)

Saturday Night Fever went on to sell 30 million albums and cassettes, making it the biggest soundtrack album of all time until Whitney Houston's 1992 soundtrack to *The Bodyguard* unseated it. Considering the elements that made the album a phenomenon—high tenor harmonies, nightlife lyrics, cutting-edge dance moves, iconic clothing—Michael Jackson must have been paying attention.

After production on *The Wiz* wrapped, Michael returned to Los Angeles. He was twenty years old and armed with a slew of musical ideas, some he'd been harboring for years and others inspired by the newest trends in dance music. Unlike many West Coast music folks, who were slow or resistant to disco, Michael had seen it, heard it, and saw the future— his future.

AUDIO/VISUAL II

I T IS SEPTEMBER 1981, AND I'M SITTING IN A FLOOR seat at Madison Square Garden alongside a woman who will become my first serious postcollege girlfriend. I have great seats because I'm the black music editor at *Record World* magazine, my first real job as a music journalist. This year I will interview Prince, Morris Day and the Time, Jermaine Jackson, Rick James, the Dramatics, and many more. A young, upcoming party promoter named Russell Simmons hosts a party for me and talks endlessly about a new genre called rap music. The world of black popular music, which has obsessed me since I was a little boy, is undergoing a profound changing of the guard that I will be lucky enough to witness.

I am finally a full-fledged working journalist. But I am also very much a fan, whose profile is the same as that of most in the crowd: black, early teens to late twenties, people for whom the Jacksons are part of their DNA. The group is performing one of thirty-six shows on its sold-out *Triumph* tour, one *Rolling Stone* would later name one of the top concerts of the 1980s. Although the tour is named after the Jacksons' latest album, in truth it should have been called the *"Off the Wall* tour featuring some cuts from *Triumph."*

IN THE FOUR YEARS BETWEEN the CBS series and this tour, the Jacksons in general, and Michael in particular, revamped their sound and image. Their once-trademark Afros gave way to the now-fashionable jheri curls, and the boys' occasional pelvic thrusts were now more sexual in nature.

After a so-so two-album apprenticeship under Philly sound mavens Kenny Gamble and Leon Huff—where the boys had one major hit, "Enjoy Yourself," while studying under the masters of the message song—the Jacksons finally took control of the writing and production. Though there were some Epic-imposed executive producers and material ("Blame It on the Boogie"), they flexed some creative muscle, with Tito, Marlon, and elder brother Jackie contributing material. With Jermaine pursuing a solo career (and staying at his father-in-law's label), the long-silent background brothers got a chance to speak. But the true revelation of *Destiny* (1978) and *Triumph* (1980) was what an accomplished songwriter Michael was, which he achieved with his chief collaborator: baby brother Randy.

In retrospect, the Garden show was significant because it was the first concert I attended where the songs were performed in the shadow of music videos. Several years before MTV's debut, NBC had a late-night show called *Friday Night Videos*, a showcase for the short music films that were made to market acts in Europe. New York DJ Frankie Crocker, trying to make a transition into television, was the show's semiregular host, his deep baritone now accompanied by the image of a slim, chic black man with a sharp nose and snazzy suit.

It was on *Friday Night Videos* that I and millions of other viewers got our first taste of how Michael saw himself. From *Off the Wall* came two videos for two great records—"Don't Stop 'Til You Get Enough" and "Rock with You." The production values of both are typical of the kind of low-budget videos that black artists would be saddled with well into the mid-1980s: on videotape before a primitive green screen where backgrounds were dropped in later. As special effects, they are deeply chintzy, even by the standards of the era.

Despite these limitations, both videos show a young man comfortable in the spotlight by himself. He is performing without props, backing dancers, or a big concept (a rare occurrence in his career). He seems to be having a good time, smiling and joyous without any of the self-consciousness, calculation, or rage of later videos.

In "Don't Stop 'Til You Get Enough," Michael wears a tuxedo, tux tie, white shirt, black shoes, and glittering socks (similar to the outfit he'd wear later in the "Billie Jean" video). For "Rock with You," Michael dons a glittering jumpsuit that looks made of the same material as his famous iridescent glove. Much has been made of the fact that Michael's dancing recalled James Brown. And although Michael and Brown did share spins and a similar intensity, Jackson also learned from Jackie Wilson, as is evident in these two videos. Though he didn't have the consistent musical success of Brown, Wilson was one of the only soul era performers who could be as dazzling onstage as the Godfather of Soul. Wilson was an ex–Golden Gloves boxer from Detroit whose footwork reflected that athletic grace. Michael watched Wilson from the wings countless times as a child and internalized much of what he saw.

The way Michael holds the microphone. The way he holds his upper body as he spins. His hand gestures with his non-microphone-holding hand. How he tilts his head and isolates his body parts as he dances. There's a bit of Wilson in all of these MJ moves. Michael's vocal range and whoops sound a lot more like Wilson's high tenor and hiccups than Brown's gritty growls. There are beautiful echoes of this old master in young Michael, a performer just defining his adult style.

After establishing his star persona on *Off the Wall,* Michael wasn't ready to become a team player again with the Jacksons. The video for "Can You Feel It," the first single from *Triumph,* had a much bigger budget and a very ambitious concept. In it, the Jacksons are godlike figures bringing light to the darkness of mankind. In pretension and iconography, this video recalls Jehovah's Witnesses scripture, where Jesus Christ raises a select number of the dead to walk again on a heavenly earth.

In the Jacksons' version of the resurrection, Michael stands front and center, his brothers flanked behind him as supporting players. Like Atlas, Michael holds a globe over his head, but this orb sends out a glowing light. His other brothers have a moment or two of omnipotence in the video, but Michael is the true redeemer. This depiction of Michael as a creature blessed with the power to transform both nature and man would become a consistent visual theme in his career.

The concert at Madison Square Garden (and all the dates on the *Triumph* tour) opened with a projection of the "Can You Feel It" video, a harbinger of Michael's involvement with mixing film and live performance. (Twenty-eight years later his star-crossed *This Is It* concert was to be filled with extensive use of video clips to augment the performance.) As the clip ended, Randy Jackson, in a suit of armor, emerged holding a flaming torch, as if the Jacksons were about to lead concertgoers out of the wilderness. For most of the show, Michael glided across the stage in a jumpsuit much like his glittering "Rock with You" outfit. Then after an explosion near the end of the show, Michael appeared on a riser in his "Don't Stop" tuxedo and the glittering socks.

THE PLAYLIST ON THE *TRIUMPH* TOUR, documented on a 1981 live album, speaks to Michael's musical domination of the group. Five of the fifteen songs are from *Off the Wall* (the title track, "She's Out of My Life," "Rock with You," "Working Day and Night," "Don't Stop 'Til You Get

Enough"). There's one old-school Michael solo song ("Ben"), and there are a number of songs either co-written or solely composed by Michael on *Destiny* or *Triumph* ("This Place Hotel," "Can You Feel It," "Lovely One," "Shake Your Body [Down to the Ground]").

Musically, Randy Jackson is also extremely prominent. Not only has Randy co-written the show closer, "Shake," but he's also the featured keyboardist on "She's Out of My Life," the concert's emotional high point. Michael, who supervised the stage design and obviously influenced the song selection, clearly trusted his little brother. Overall, Michael was much closer to his young siblings (Randy and Janet) than to his older brothers, with whom he rarely collaborated musically.

With the exception of "This Place Hotel," which features a dynamic, rhythmic guitar solo, dramatic brass arrangement, and a chamber music coda, the Jacksons' material isn't as intricately arranged as the songs on *Off the Wall*. "Things I Do for You," "Lovely One," and "Shake" are built around strong riffs but harmonically and rhythmically aren't as interesting as "Rock with You," "Off the Wall," or "Don't Stop 'Til You Get Enough." There is a richness to the musical palate of the Quincy Jones–produced tracks that's clear even in concert.

What holds all the material from these different albums together is Michael's voice, which is why this live album is so valuable. It allows us to study his instrument outside a recording studio (though Michael, perfectionist that he was becoming, probably overdubbed at least a line or two). What you hear is that almost the entire vocabulary of Michael's mature vocal mannerisms are already in place. On "This Place Hotel," the "whoo-hoos" that would become one of his trademarks are in place, used as transitions between lines in verses and occasionally before or after choruses. Hiccups are employed liberally on the song, as are the trademark "he he hees." Just as the song's paranoid subject matter and production point toward Michael's future, so does Michael's vocal approach, which makes this performance a preview of greatest hits to come.

On "She's Out of My Life," keyboardist-arranger Tom Bahler's look back at his failed relationship with singer Karen Carpenter, Michael sings carefully, with great respect for the lyric's meaning and lots of soft vibrato. He holds phrases like "laugh or cry" and "live or die" by extending, but never distorting, them. The performance is looser than his dramatic interpretation on the *Off the Wall* album (where Michael cried after every take), but works beautifully for the screaming girls in the crowd.

At the end of a medley of Jackson 5 hits, the Jacksons launch into "I'll Be There," which Michael sings in a light, confident manner well supported by his brothers' harmonies. Like on the record, the performance is very controlled until the end, when Michael becomes the kid who could convincingly sing like Ray Charles. He begins by extending the words, adding a serious church preacher vibe that excites the crowd before flowing into his "he he hees" and then a run of percussive vocal sounds like a violin being plucked by nimble fingers.

This fun riffing then leads Michael to say, "I wanna rock," and drummer Jonathan Moffett kicks off the groove of "Rock with You." However, the missing vocal element in this performance is aggression. Whereas soul music encouraged a rough, nasty-edge quality in its singers, Michael's R&B style utilized elements of that old edge, but balanced it with his natural sweetness and feel for rhythm. The new music Michael was recording didn't really demand that he tap into that gritty side of himself. Neither of the two Jacksons albums or *Off the Wall* featured songs of a traditional soul structure, probably because it was increasingly anachronistic in the 1980s.

Guitars play a prominent role in much of this new music, but the riffs played here by Tito and the supporting band are mostly rhythm. Even the guitar solo on "Heartbreak Hotel," while tasty, doesn't have the roughness of rock. So Michael had yet to record anything in this new phase of his career that pushed him vocally or musically in a more aggressive direction. Despite the success of this show, Michael Joe Jackson was still a work in progress.

BLACK
HOLLYWOOD

T'S THE EARLY 1980S, AND I AM IN THE OFFICES OF Joe Jackson's management company, located in the Motown building at 6255 Sunset Boulevard, a holdover from the days when the Jackson family functioned as a subsidiary of Berry Gordy's legendary enterprise. Jackson-mania is well under way, and Joe, though no longer Michael's day-to-day manager, still has access to his most famous son.

I'm with Joe to talk about a few topics, including the careers of his daughters Janet and LaToya. Janet, signed to A&M Records, is not yet a major pop star, and LaToya, who would release an album on PolyGram, hadn't yet made a spectacle of herself or married poorly. Joe is a formidable figure with a mane of hair around his head that, along with his piercing, hooded eyes, suggests that Joe is part man, part lion king, a perception encouraged by the lion statuette sitting on his desk.

At some point in the conversation, Joe feels he has to prove his continuing closeness to Michael. So he picks up the phone, punches in a number, and begins talking. "I have the writer from *Billboard* here. Nelson George, yeah." Then he hands me the receiver.

Michael Jackson sounds as uncomfortable as I feel. I tell him it's a pleasure to talk with him, though Michael's short, low-energy reply makes it clear the feeling is not mutual. I awkwardly try to engage him in conversation and ask for a face-to-face interview. Dead air.

Joe takes the receiver from me, and my only direct conversation with Michael Jackson is over. Perhaps if Joe hadn't bullied Michael into talking with me, maybe I would have eventually gotten some quality time with MJ. Or maybe he just wasn't interested. So while the content of the talk was feeble, the context of that brief conversation was rich, a real window into the relationship between father and son. Joe wanted to prove he could still get in touch with Michael anytime he wanted, no matter how much that imposed on his son's privacy. For Michael this forced conversation was likely just another of the innumerable indignities that the star would become fed up with, one of the many reasons that decades later Joe was left out of his son's will.

This display of power by Joe was one of many intimate moments with the Jacksons' circle I'd experience during the period from 1981 to 1985, when Michael and the folks around him were central to the story of American popular music. I'd meet a lot of people who would give insight into the world that made Michael and the world Michael would make.

"LOS ANGELES IS DEFINED by vast geographical distances and the cars needed to travel them, by sun and smog, by beauty and a tacky squalor almost redeemed by the absence of cold," wrote music critic John Rockwell of the sound of Hollywood in the late 1970s. "The distances and the general lack of high culture (it exists but has to be sought out) have bred a sense of isolation, not just of the various communities that make up the Los Angeles basin but of the individuals and especially the creative individuals within these communities."

Focusing on the music business, Rockwell added: "Socializing thus tends to be cliquish, like-minded souls seeking one another out and guarding what they share against the environment. People congregate in recording studios or at ritualized industry functions, and it's possible to go for what seems like years without meeting anyone who doesn't reinforce your own longstanding opinions."

When Berry Gordy shifted Motown's operations from Detroit to Los Angeles in the early 1970s, he did more than nurture the Jackson 5. He changed the geographic balance of power in black pop. Just as Detroit had Motown, other cities with substantial African American populations (Philadelphia, Chicago, Memphis, Atlanta, New Orleans, Cincinnati) all had local labels that supported homegrown entertainers.

LA and New York had always been major destinations, but Motown's move west, coupled with the major labels jumping deeply into black music in the 1970s, meant that an aspiring artist had to be in either city to find session work, network with industry figures, and get signed to a label. So along with Marvin Gaye, Stevie Wonder, Smokey Robinson, and the musicians and staff Motown employed, future big names such as Chicago's Maurice White (founder of Earth, Wind and Fire), Tulsa's Charlie Wilson (lead singer of the Gap Band), and midwesterners Antonio Reid and Kenny Edmonds (future hit-making producer/writers) relocated out west because that's where the action was.

This shift coincided with two other black pop phenomena: blaxploitation movies featuring black storylines, creating black stars (Pam Grier, Fred Williamson), and driven by dynamic funk soundtracks; and Don Cornelius's *Soul Train*, a syndicated black dance show that gave a regular national profile to black artists, style, and dance. At the same time, there was an influx of black kids into the private and public schools of the Hollywood elite. Jackie, who was the oldest and the best athlete, fit in best, playing sports and chasing girls with easy charm. Jermaine, Marlon, and Tito all enjoyed the bubble of pseudonormalcy that LA can provide for celebrities and their offspring. Michael, being young and shy, and already a star among stars, didn't mix very easily or very well, his childlike voice the object of ridicule from friends and family alike. That he had pimples and didn't play sports didn't help his social life either. Nevertheless, through his more outgoing brothers, Michael socialized with and met scores of folks and created a few enduring friendships.

One of the kids who became part of the Jackson boys' circle was John McClain, a lean, handsome young man whose mother was jazz pianist Shirley Scott and whose father owned a string of funeral homes around LA. McClain hung with the Jacksons as they evolved from a kiddie pop group into a young adult band. McClain himself played several instruments but would make his name as a record executive.

McClain joined A&M Records in the early 1980s as an A&R executive and would sign Janet to a record deal when she was sixteen. I met John around this time, just before he hooked the youngest Jackson daughter up with Jimmy Jam and Terry Lewis and created the Jackson family's second superstar.

After Michael's death, the name John McClain became known to those closely following the battle over the estate because, along with Jackson's former attorney John Branca, McClain was named in Michael's will as an executor of his estate. Unlike Branca, who's always been a very visible figure in the Hollywood entertainment firmament, John hasn't spoken to the media in years and has appeared in very few photographs over the last decade.

Back in the mid-1980s, John was an emerging figure in the black music business and something of a friend of mine. He was a soft-spoken dude with a sly sense of humor and a very generous soul. He was part of a tightly knit community of executives, managers, and attorneys who either grew up in LA or had moved there post-Motown. Before Prince became a superstar and hip-hop emerged as a national commercial force, this group really set the direction for black pop music.

The Motown building on Sunset Boulevard, right across from the historic Hollywood Palladium concert hall and two blocks from the famed Cineramadome, was a nexus for the black music community, as non-Motown folks, from accountants to publicists to managers, moved into the building or into the area around it. A homely little black-owned spot named Roscoe's Chicken and Waffles, on Gower one block from the Motown building, became a major black entertainment business lunch spot and today is a classic LA eatery.

The values of the LA community were very different from those I knew in New York, where disco was losing steam, the city was recovering from a fiscal crisis, and crime was rampant. Sure, there was gritty street life in LA, but not where black Hollywood hung. At Carlos and Charlie's, a two-story Sunset Strip nightclub, you'd find Eddie Murphy, Hollywood's hottest young star, along with his posse of homeboys (known jokingly as the A Team) and lots of gorgeous groupies. Rick James, Jim Brown, and a young Prince were among the regulars you'd spot in a booth upstairs.

At Carlos and Charlie's or at a happening Hollywood Hills party, moist California curls, tenaciously teased new wavy hair, young black folks in Corvette convertibles, and girls in dresses so short they'd have been illegal in several states were on display. Living a sun-kissed existence created an R&B aesthetic that celebrated smooth over raw, shiny studio perfection over raunchy funk. There were some important exceptions (the Gap Band on LA- based Total Experience Records, some of Leon Sylvers's production at Sound of Los Angeles Records), but no one mistook the early 1980s sound of black pop for Booker T. and the MGs. Contributing to this change was growing use of computer technology. Bands such as Earth, Wind and Fire, Cameo, and Con Funk Shun, all featuring horn sections and several percussion instruments, replaced human players with synthesizers and drum machines.

In this social and musical context, Michael Jackson's collaborations with Quincy Jones, starting with *Off the Wall* in 1979, were as important for his development as a Hollywood player as for his work as a musician. Quincy was one of the few prominent African American figures in Hollywood in the years before Motown arrived. After a distinguished career as a jazz arranger, bandleader, and record executive, Quincy moved to LA and became one of the few black composers to work regularly in Hollywood.

Aside from working on movies such as *The Anderson Tapes,* Quincy penetrated the popular consciousness by penning TV themes for *Ironside, The Bill Cosby Show, Sanford and Son,* and the historic *Roots* miniseries. He married one of the 1960s hottest blonds, Peggy Lipton of *Mod Squad* fame, and became a popular guest at Hollywood parties, where he and actor Sidney Poitier were often the only blacks in attendance. He was a popular presence at the Grammys, the Oscars, and every other major event on the LA social calendar.

The Wiz was the fourth score Quincy had composed or supervised for director Sidney Lumet. Aside from introducing
Michael to genius engineer Bruce Swedien and a powerhouse community of musicians Quincy had already worked
with (the Brothers Johnson, members of Rufus) during the
sessions of *Off the Wall,* Quincy opened up his wider circle of
relationships to Michael. It was Quincy who brought Paul
McCartney's "Girlfriend" to the sessions and who introduced
Michael to the ex-Beatle, fostering a relationship that would
pay big dividends for Michael and foreshadow his entry into
the pop music pantheon.

PART 2

THRILLER

I N THE AGE OF DOWNLOADS AND ITUNES, I STILL own lots of vinyl, including hundreds of albums and count-less 45 rpm singles, some of which I liberated decades ago from my mother's once-vast record collection. I treasure them all, even if I haven't played any of them in years. The albums sit high on a white bookshelf, and one level down, in milk crates, are my battered, almost ancient, singles. I have a digital turntable, which I received as a gift, with great enthu-siasm, thinking I'd turn all my vinyl into MP3 files. But that technological transfer has fallen victim to my schedule, so mostly my albums sit on their shelf, giving me old-school cred while collecting dust.

On this day I walk over to the pile and, as a young DJ might say, start "diggin'" for a particular album. There's a tac-tile pleasure in navigating through the pile, a connection to the not-too-distant past when many of my days involved looking for an LP I really wanted to hear. It was an act of physical labor, sometimes fun, sometimes frustrating, to find that special combo of cardboard and vinyl calling out to you. Finally, I find the album and slide it out of the pile.

In a white suit with pleated pants, black-zippered shirt, and leopard-print handkerchief and coiffed with a nicely backlit jheri curl, Michael Jackson gazes out from the cover of *Thriller.* His name and the title are written in a quirky script. The gatefold album cover opens up to reveal a lounging Michael Jackson balancing a baby cougar on his right knee.

On the back are the song titles, written in the same script, along with the production and management credits. On the inner sleeve are the lyrics to every song (actually readable, unlike inner-sleeve copy in the coming CD age) and two of the many pen-and-ink drawings the singer rendered during *Thriller*'s production. On side one Michael and Paul McCartney pull at a very skinny woman in a re-creation of the lyrics of "The Girl Is Mine." On the other side Michael and a strangely haired friend (who looks more like a child than the vivacious Ola Ray of the video) are watching Frankenstein and other monsters escape the screen to surround them. The cartoons give this very-well-designed 1980s record package an endearingly idiosyncratic touch.

In fact, I could use similar words to describe *Thriller*'s music: a very-well-designed 1980s package with enough idiosyncratic touches to make it seem an individual statement. This album is both a calculated commercial product and a projection of a singular, cartoony, passionate, odd, dreamy, anxious individual, enabled by a crew of skilled artists and craftsmen.

Both God and the Devil can be found in the details. Almost all significant cultural expressions, no matter how elaborate the final presentation or how global the reach, are created in little rooms, often dark, small, definitely out of the way, and usually grimy. Great work is created in a tedious accumulation of raindrops that its creator hopes will eventually become a powerful storm of art.

In previous centuries, the cliché was that an artist worked in damp basements or cold attics, he or she chipping at stone or sliding a brush stroke across a tall canvas. The twenty-first century version is a bedroom lined with laptops and digital equipment as the artist hopes to one day upload something of emotional and commercial value after too many days of takeout Chinese food. *Thriller* was recorded from April to October 1982 at one of the state-of-the-art studios of the predigital era: Westlake Studios, a nondescript building where glittery LA pop was created. Wood-paneled walls held gold and platinum records, a lounge held a color TV, and there was a kitchen for coffee, tea, and expensive takeout from places like Mr. Chow. As in Vegas casinos, there were few clocks visible, only timepieces that monitored the length of tracks being cut.

Westlake was located on Beverly Boulevard, just a few blocks from the Beverly Center, which in the 1980s was the preeminent shopping mall in Los Angeles county, a place where people went to meet as much as shop. Every New

Yorker I knew stopped by the Beverly Center when in LA whenever he or she was suffering from the sensory under-load of the town's car culture. I know because I made my first trip to Los Angeles in 1981 and would become a regular visitor to LA, the Beverly Center, and Westlake Studios, where I'd conduct a number of interviews with Quincy Jones and his creative associates in the years before and after the explosion that was *Thriller*. In the pages that follow, I'm gonna lean a lot on some of those twenty-five-plus-year-old conversations because they bring me back to that time with-out the haze of nostalgia or the smooth glow of revisionism.

THERE ARE SEVERAL WAYS to look at the biggest-selling record of all time, a prime artifact of the early years of block-buster American culture. Like *Roots* on television (which Quincy scored) and *Star Wars* in movie theaters, both in 1977, *Thriller* redefined how big and culturally binding a commercial entertainment product could be. The album eclipsed the sales of all that had come before and set an un-reachable mark for recordings to come. A success this mas-sive can be seen retrospectively not only as the beginning of something but also as the end of an era. *Thriller* was both.

Thriller was one of the last predigital (analog) albums. It proved to be the apex of decades of striving by black artists for mainstream acceptance. The album set unrealistic expec-tations for what black music success could be. It confirmed that music videos in general, and MTV in particular, would be as important as radio and record companies for popular music during the next twenty-five years. It reconnected the history of rock 'n' roll to the narrative of black popular music. It brought an African influence to the pop charts. It contained songs whose videos were more enduring than the often-mediocre music that generated them. It epitomized the pop craftsmanship of Los Angeles session cats while supporting the playful nightmares of its star. It was the high point for a record industry that is now as weak as the auto industry, though for Sony, Warner Music, Universal, and the rest, there is no government bailout in sight.

In spring 1982, I traveled to Westlake Studios to meet with forty-nine-year-old maestro Quincy Delight Jones Jr. (I did a major interview for *Musician* magazine, and the cover subject of the September 1982 issue in which the interview was published was guitarist Eddie Van Halen.) Quincy was the most charming man I'd ever met, uncannily able to put me at ease and to make me like him and want to please him. Within ten minutes of meeting him at Westlake, he'd told me my writing reminded him of a best-selling author. I don't even remember the author's name, but the idea that Quincy was paying that much attention flattered me. Given the range of talent he's worked with—Frank Sinatra, Leslie Gore, Dinah Washington, Michael Jackson—I've always thought that his greatest gift, even more than his musical acumen, is this charm.

"What kind of man is able to deal with such a wide variety of music?" I wrote.

Well, for one thing, a man who lives in Los Angeles, the car craziest town in America, and doesn't drive. . . . [He] has the cool, hip quality associated with veterans of the be-bop era. Words like "cat" and "man" flow easily from his mouth, as do references to pretty women, hanging out and the urban street life that you'd expect from someone years his junior. That youthful vitality, tempered by a wisdom acquired the hard way, are strong elements of Jones's personality and both are definitely felt in his music.

Digital recording technology was already making inroads in studios in 1982, but Quincy wasn't yet a fan. *Thriller* would be recorded at the crux of the transition from analog to digital, with its feet firmly on the old-school side of the fence. In producing George Benson's *Give Me the Night*, Quincy and engineer Bruce Swedien had utilized some digital equipment, but for the Donna Summer album he was finishing when we talked and the Michael Jackson album he was about to dive into, analog tech would dominate. "It [digital] will be ready soon," he observed, "but it still has to be developed to deal with all the characteristics of sound. It scans the sounds and analyzes them scientifically, but it loses unscientific sounds. There is a build up and dirt that you want that it eliminates. It's too clean and I don't want my music to sound like that because it's not conceived that way. Music is conceived in passion and should sound like it."

In later years, there'd be some confusion over who played on what *Thriller* track. Drummer Ndugu Chancler has always claimed that he, not Jeff Porcaro, played drums on "Human Nature." On the original pressings of the album, Dean Parks was listed as the guitar player on "Billie Jean" when David Williams actually did the playing. Much of this confusion over the credits was due to Swedien's approach to engineering *Thriller*.

He used two twenty-four-track tape machines to record and often four to five reels of tape per song, which the album notes called the Acoustic Recording Process. This often translated into one hundred tracks per song, a fantastic number of options for a producer and a nightmare for someone tabulating musicians' credits. Once the rhythm tracks were recorded, Swedien ran off work tapes with a cue mix and put the masters away until the final mix, minimizing sonic wear and tear.

Quincy and I talked a lot about the producer's role in record-making and his relationship with the artist he's producing. Quincy told me:

> The producer has to be concerned also with an overall vision that comes organically from what the artist is all about, their essence. I don't believe that the artist necessarily has to agree with how you perceive them. Sometimes it is very difficult for them to understand what they're about and the things they haven't tried. They know very well what they've done before, but not the new things.
>
> The smallest, tiniest detail can make a tremendous difference. You don't indiscriminately put on a horn part, a

percussion part or a guitar part. I've been in a recording studio thirty-two years. By now I understand intuitively that there are certain things you can put on a record to create an illusion or an emotion. You can't pile things on. You can put a lot of things on a record and the listeners will never hear them. You have to have a big vision of the entire project. . . . You have to have more and more enthusiasm, not less, as time goes on. By the time you're mixing, you have to have more enthusiasm than when you started.

At the time we were talking, Quincy had already started working on *Thriller*, wading through the hundreds of songs he and Michael were considering for inclusion. Quincy was, of course, highly complimentary of his chief collaborator:

He is the essence of what a performer and an artist are all about. Michael has got all you need emotionally, but he backs it up with discipline and pacing. . . . Oh man, he'd come in during *Off the Wall* and put down two lead vocals and three background parts in one day. He does his homework and rehearses and works hard at home. Most singers want to do everything in the studio. They're lazy.

When he commits to an idea, he goes all the way with it. He has the presence of mind to feel something, conceive it and then bring it to life. It's a long way from idea to execution. Everybody wants to go to heaven and nobody wants to die. It's ass power, man. You have to be emotionally ready to put as much energy into it as it takes to make it right.

If *Off the Wall* represented Michael's maturation into young manhood, *Thriller* fully fleshed out a theme in his writing and singing that had already peeked out in the Jacksons albums. As Michael became a man, anger became as prominent a part of his work as his oft-mentioned childlike quality. Between *Off the Wall* and *Thriller,* Michael found a fierce, judgmental, and combative voice. The paranoia that "This Place Hotel" had revealed was given free reign on this record. (When Michael's vocal range lowered slightly with age, he found a new sweet spot that spoke to his displeasure with media, family, women, and the endless legion of users he'd encountered.)

LYRICALLY, THREE KEY SONGS ("Wanna Be Startin' Somethin'," "Billie Jean," and "Beat It") constitute Jackson's personal trilogy of terror, revisiting some earlier ideas and introducing themes that would recur throughout his work. The evil women of "Heartbreak Hotel" have returned in the form of one treacherous gal named Billie Jean, who torments Michael, accusing him of fathering her son. In "Startin' Somethin'," another woman (perhaps the same one?) spreads lies and uses her body as a weapon to upset Michael's "baby" and cause pain.

In both songs, Michael sings with great anger and palpable paranoia about being observed, talked about, and desired. In "Billie Jean," he recalls his mother's advice to be careful about whom you love because of the ease with which lies are confused with truth. His fear of the outside world, and its designs upon him, lead him to compare his body to a buffet and then a vegetable that "they" (media, father, family, record business) feast on. He reinforces that notion on "Beat It," noting that given a chance, "they" will attack you physically and mentally and still justify their actions. Taken coldly, without Michael's voice giving these sentiments dimension, these ideas may seem less than profound, but, of course, his voice gives them depth.

Children play a prominent role in "Startin' Somethin'" and "Billie Jean," but not as the objects of joy Michael spoke of so often. The little boy in "Billie Jean" is the result of an affair Michael regrets. In "Startin' Somethin'," he bluntly states that people shouldn't have a baby if they can't feed the child, a pragmatic and unromantic view of sex. Such comments might be traced to the Jehovah's Witnesses tenets that Michael learned from his mother, a group that makes stern admonitions against premarital sex. The very moralistic, conservative view of the world embedded in this wondrous pop music was as fearful of the modern world as was the neoconservative movement ascendant at the time of *Thriller*'s release.

The irony is that musically speaking Michael is totally progressive, always pushing for sounds and approaches different from what came before. It is this tension between his old-fashioned morality, his fear of the outside world, and his artistic boldness that makes these three songs such enormous achievements.

I'm going to look at each song on *Thriller* track by track in the order it appears on the disc. Sometimes I'll be doing a close reading of the production and lyrics, sometimes looking both backward and forward in time, seeing how some of the songs comment on the pop music that came before and how others altered (or didn't) the music that came after. Also, since Michael's untimely death, many of the songs have taken on renewed, or in some cases new, cultural relevance. In the continuing dialogue over what Michael means and what his legacy is, as both artist and man, *Thriller* should be the central point of reference.

"WANNA BE STARTIN' SOMETHIN'"

O NE OF THE MOST IMPORTANT BY-PRODUCTS of the late 1960s was a building of bonds between Africa and the newly named "black" Americans, folks who just a few years before had been known as Negroes. The phrase "Black is beautiful" spoke to the transformation of a people's sense of identity that had many profound manifestations. One of the best was an earnest, if sometimes naïve, identification with Africa, a continent that black Americans had been physically and psychologically separated from by white racism for generations.

The *Tarzan* films and thousands of other equally racist movie depictions of Africans as savage cannibals easily outwitted by white folks and in need of white folks to save them were commonplace. It took a great act of collective will to begin the long process of breaking the mental shackles that made black Americans ashamed of their skin. Africa, in truth, was a land of ancient cultures and traditions blacks knew little about in the 1960s and early 1970s.

Music was the most obvious link between two peoples who'd been separated by slavery and centuries. Consequently, several multiact American soul music concerts were organized and, thankfully, recorded and filmed. The "Soul to Soul" concert was held in Accra, Ghana, in 1971 and featured a smart mix of jazzy soul acts (Roberta Flack, Les McCann, Eddie Harris), unconventional Latin musicians (Santana, Willie Bobo), and straight-up soul power singers (the Staple Singers, Ike and Tina Turner) who performed before 100,000 people. Ike Turner, whose extraordinary skills as a bandleader have been overshadowed by his abuse of Tina Turner, was quite moving in his reactions to visiting the motherland.

James Brown, whose funk was the crucial influence on the creation of West African Afro-beat music, ventured to Africa several times in the 1970s, most famously as part of a concert to accompany the 1974 "Rumble in the Jungle" championship bout between Muhammad Ali and George Foreman in Kinshasa, Zaire. The strong lineup included Bill Withers, the Spinners, the Fania All-Stars featuring Cecila Cruz, B. B. King, and Miriam Makeba. It took twenty-two years for the documentary of this historic heavyweight battle, *When We Were Kings*, to reach theaters. It took another thirteen years for *Soul Power*, the documentary record of those concerts and the performers' interaction with local musicians and fans, to be completed.

One memorable scene in *Soul Power* follows Manu Dibango, a Cameroonian saxophonist, as he plays for a dancing, adoring group of children. Dibango, who had a strong following throughout West Africa, was able to achieve worldwide pop success, at the time a rare occurrence, which was very much tied up with the rise of disco. His 1972 recording "Soul Makossa" was the B side of another single and surely would have remained obscure if not for David Mancuso, a visionary New York DJ, who threw legendary parties in a lower Manhattan loft. The party itself became known as the Loft and featured Mancuso, with his turntable in the center of the room, playing an eclectic mix of dance records that attracted a lively cult audience, one that veterans of the New York club scene argue created the first disco music experience. Mancuso, who was the first to play many songs now regarded as disco classics, found Dibango's record in a West Indian record store in Brooklyn.

"Soul Makossa" might have remained a cult item if Frankie Crocker, the adventurous WBLS program director and DJ, hadn't heard it at Mancuso's party and put it on the air in New York City. By 1973 "Soul Makossa" had become a minimania, with some thirty cover versions being recorded, while Dibango's original went on to reach number thirty-five on the pop chart. This musical journey, from progressive New York disco to WBLS playlist to international success, would be replayed scores of times during the disco era.

COMPARED TO "SOUL TO SOUL" and *Soul Power,* the Jackson 5's pilgrimage to Africa in 1973 was much more modest. At the urging of promoter Mamadu Johnny Seeka and with the backing of the government, three shows were organized in Senegal, West Africa, as were trips to villages, official ceremonies, and the ancient slave deportation site on Goree Island. Joe, Michael, Jackie, Tito, Jermaine, and young Randy, who was apprenticing on congas, landed in Dakar late at night and were greeted by drummers, dancers, and cheering fans.

But for activist Johnny Seeka, this trip was as much about education as it was about entertainment. The same was true for the documentary he planned, the footage of which was lost for decades, only resurfacing after Michael Jackson's death. At a Harlem screening organized by ImageNation, a community-oriented African American film exhibition company, on July 14, 2009, a packed house viewed a print of *The Jackson 5 in Africa,* a film rarely seen in the United States.

The film, narrated by popular black TV actor Robert Hooks, is a straight-up piece of black nationalist propaganda. It uses the Jackson family's visit to give viewers a primer on postcolonial African politics, the cultural connections between blacks and Africans, and the need for more investment in Africa by its stolen peoples.

The print screened that night in Harlem was in terrible shape. There were numerous frames with sound but no image. Sometimes the sound was in sync and sometimes not, which was particularly frustrating during the concert footage.

Apparently, all the shows were shot with one camera, so most of the concerts were shot in wide masters, with some occasional pans and zooms. Compared to a beautifully photographed documentary such as *Soul Power,* the film was a frustrating mess. (By the end of 2009, a color-corrected trailer of *The Jackson 5 in Africa* was up on YouTube, but there was no word of a formal release.)

But the film does give some depth to the photographs and stories from that trip. Photographer Kwame Braithwaite, who was also a political activist in Harlem, accompanied the Jacksons and observed: "The poverty they saw there seemed to really bother them. Gary, Indiana, is not a rich city, but they had never seen people live as they are forced to live in Africa."

The trip to the slave quarters at Goree Island, a holding area where chained Africans were kept before boarding ships for the Middle Passage to the Caribbean and the Americas, was especially jarring for the Jacksons. "I studied Goree in high school and college," Jackie Jackson later said, "but I never did know exactly what it was like until I came over here and saw. I never did know the places were that small or how they captured them and chained them up like that."

Michael Jackson was fourteen years old in 1974, a lanky, pimply adolescent wearing geeky white sweaters as he walked through African villages, visited Goree, and listened to the drummers of Senegal play. During these experiences, he felt a swelling sense of racial pride. "I always thought that blacks, as far as artistry, were the most talented race on earth.

But when I went to Africa, I was even more convinced. They do incredible things there. They've got the beats and rhythm. I really see where drums come from. . . . I don't want the blacks to ever forget that this is where we come from and where our music comes from. I want us to remember."

MEMORY HAS ALWAYS BEEN a crucial tool for a pop musician, even before the current era of sampling. Remembering older songs and mining them for riffs or harmonies are how new songs are often inspired and created. On the demo of "Wanna Be Startin' Somethin'," the melody, Michael's vocal approach, and the rhythm shifts that made the final song a dance classic are already in place, even though the demo is clearly still a work in progress.

But the use of the African chant "*Mama-se, mama-sa, mama-coo-sa*," which lifts the record up and sends it soaring, is still being worked out. About three minutes into the song, the phrase pops up awkwardly and then disappears. That happens again about thirty seconds later, before Michael and his background singers sing this hook full on during the last forty-five seconds of the demo. These voices perform over a collage of percussion instruments that are much more African sounding than in the dynamic final version.

When you compare Dibango's superfunky original, "Soul Makossa" (from the Cameroonian dance the *kossa,* which evolved into a regional genre of music called *Makossa*), and the final version of Michael's song, you get a deep insight into Michael's musicality. He arranges the words in a much higher key and at a faster rhythm, turning Dibango's monotone delivery into a high-spirited chant. Up until the last bridge, the song's lyric presents a paranoid vision of the world. Michael reshapes Dibango's old hook, turning the fear in the song's first two-thirds into an inspired celebration.

Dibango called his song "Soul Makossa" to make it sound more Western and modern. Though not credited as a cowriter on "Wanna," Dibango did make a financial settlement with Jackson's camp, a good investment for all involved because the *makossa* phrase would continue to appear in the twenty-first century. Rihanna used a version of the chant in her 2007 smash "Don't Stop the Music." Via Michael Jackson and Rihanna, that West African cadence has now filled dance floors around the globe for four decades.

On August 29, 2009, on what would have been Michael Jackson's fifty-first birthday, filmmaker Spike Lee invited a few friends to help him celebrate. Spike had great affection for Michael, having directed not one but two videos for Jackson's "They Don't Care About Us" in 2007, and even had him over for a meeting in Fort Greene. On the flyer was an angelic photo of young Michael Jackson with a halo around his Afro. An estimated 20,000 men, women, and children, including lots of babies in strollers, turned up in Prospect Park to dance, dance, dance to Michael's music. Spike, who's always loved giving parties, distributed hundreds of signs with the words *Ma ma say ma ma sa mama ma kosa* to the crowd.

So toward the day's end, when DJ Spinna played "Wanna Be Startin' Somethin'," the already festive throng grew frenzied, waving the signs like church ladies fanning in a Baptist church. In Nike sneakers, flip-flops, Birkenstocks, and bare feet, thousands of Brooklynites leaped up and down, twisting and turning as the magical chant filled the air. Michael was dead. Senegal and Cameroon were an ocean away. But at that moment, Brooklyn was as connected to Africa as it could ever be.

"BABY BE MINE"

THIS SONG, WRITTEN BY THE SOMETIMES IN-
spired, often formulaic, hardworking British subject
Rod Temperton, is probably the least interesting tune
on *Thriller*. This typical R&B song probably was not good
enough to have made it onto the more-dance-oriented *Off the
Wall*. It's nowhere close to the level of "Rock with You," an
R&B groove classic Temperton had written for that album.

The songwriter had been a member of Heatwave, an integrated soul band with members from the United States and
Britain. Temperton, born and raised in England, was a student of black music; he became adept at crafting songs in a
variety of tempos with rock-solid melodic structure and very
generic lyrics. In 1976 Heatwave released a classic twelve-
inch with "The Groove Line," a well-made, guitar-based
dance record, on one side and a beautiful slow jam, "Always
and Forever," on the other. Johnnie Wilder, Heatwave's lead

singer, gave a remarkable performance that still creates a romantic aura whenever it's played.

Wilder's vocals elevated "Always and Forever," but Temperton's understanding of the genre built the platform for that performance. This skill attracted Quincy to Temperton's songs and made the Englishman part of Quincy's creative team. "I heard the Heatwave records and I had to look at them like an X-ray to figure out what it was that so knocked me out about them," he told me in 1982.

> After listening enough, I could see that it was the vision of this one guy, a complete songwriter, not like too many I've heard before. He has a natural intuitive feeling for counterpoint, not even knowing what it is. That is one of the things that really hold it together. I think that is dealing with pop music on a very high level. Without getting too heady about it, counterpoint adds another strong element to a pop song.
>
> [Temperton] will not stop until it works. Sometimes he gives me fifty titles on a song. I love a writer who explores all the possibilities and get[s] into it. It's too easy to just get a couple of ditties together and throw it down. "Take it or leave it," they say. A lot of writers do that. I can't deal with that because it's not enough commitment.

WHITE SONGWRITERS HAVE had a place in the world of R&B since the 1950s, when the writing duo of Jerry Leiber and Mike Stoller composed a string of classic songs. The late

1970s saw many white songwriters working in the black pop space, which, depending on point of view, was a golden era for the music or a low point in its history. From 1977 to 1979, white songwriters won the Grammy Award for R&B song of the year: Boz Scaggs and David Paich for "Lowdown" (recorded by Scaggs), Leo Sayer and Vini Poncia for "You Make Me Feel like Dancing" (recorded by Sayer), and Paul Jabara for "Last Dance" (recorded by Donna Summer).

Scaggs's track was a smooth, lightly funk groove with a very casual-sounding melody, a great bridge, and a lovely keyboard riff that was as cool as anything on the radio then or now. A year later, Sayer's "You Make Me Feel like Dancing" was a cute disco-influenced ditty by a lightweight white British singer with a curly Afro. It had been a major pop hit and had even generated some cursory black radio play. But that it was awarded R&B record of the year over four enduring classics—"Don't Leave Me This Way" (by Kenny Gamble, Leon Huff, and Cary Gilbert), "Easy" (by Lionel Richie), "Brick House" (by Richie with the rest of the Commodores), and "Best of My Love" (by Earth, Wind and Fire's Maurice White and Al McKay)—was a travesty.

Not quite as horrible, but in retrospect still quite silly, was Jabara's win with "Last Dance," which was given the Grammy over Gamble and Huff's soulful "Use ta Be My Girl," written for the O'Jays, and Maurice White, Verdine White, and Eddie Del Barrio's clever "Fantasy," for their band, Earth, Wind and Fire. These wins said a great deal about how the record industry viewed black pop music in the late 1970s, attitudes that Michael Jackson would be responding to with *Thriller.*

During the mid-1970s, when R&B became interchangeable with dreaded disco for many in and out of the industry, respect for black popular music took a serious nosedive. Whereas the early 1970s of Marvin Gaye, Curtis Mayfield, Sly Stone, Stevie Wonder, and so many other giants had been a golden era, later in the decade black musical culture became less ambitious. Dance music was the in thing, which wasn't necessarily bad (black music had always been dance music), but some awful records by major acts (ever hear Aretha's disco album?) and the primacy of producers over self-contained singer-songwriters made old fans of the music, black as well as white, turn their back on it. The sad truth of the period is that many black performers, either by choice or at the suggestion of record executives or managers, were altering their music, thinking disco-flavored tracks were the key to pop acceptance, even as this choice alienated so many of their traditional fans.

The membership of the National Academy of Recording Arts and Sciences (aka the Grammy voters) were not only overwhelmingly white, but were also the very people ghettoizing black music in their day jobs. Throughout the 1970s, when Earth, Wind and Fire was arguably the best band in popular music, genre be damned, it did not get enough wins in the R&B (or pop) category during the band's peak years. The same was the case with Lionel Richie during his Commodore years and seminal bands such as Parliament-

Funkadelic. The wins of Sayer and Jabara in particular, and Scaggs to a lesser degree, were graphic examples of this massive disrespect.

Unsurprisingly, then, Michael Jackson's *Off the Wall*, which had sold 11 million copies and reflected the maturation of a major star, received no Grammy nominations in any pop categories. "My pride in the rhythms, the technical advances and the success of 'Off the Wall' was offset by the jolt I got when the Grammy nominations were announced for 1979," he wrote. "Although 'Off the Wall' had been one of the most popular records of the year, it received only one nomination: Best R&B Vocal Performance [for the single]. I remember where I was when I got the news. I felt ignored by my peers and it hurt. . . . I watched the ceremony on television and it was nice to win in my category, but I was still upset by what I perceived as the rejection of my peers."

Despite the great songs Quincy and Michael had collected, and the quality of Michael's vocals, *Off the Wall* was consigned to the dance ghetto by the industry's voters. The challenge that Quincy and Michael confronted in designing *Thriller* was how to move their music, figuratively and literally, out to the suburbs. "Baby Be Mine," one of the most conventional tracks on the album, wouldn't do much to help the process. Not surprisingly, it was one of the few songs on the album not released as a single.

"THE GIRL IS MINE"

IT'S SOMETIMES OVERLOOKED THAT THE BEATLES' musical foundation was black music, particularly mid-1950s rock and roll (John Lennon) and early 1960s rhythm and blues (Paul McCartney). In January 1964, *Introducing . . . the Beatles,* the group's first U.S. album, was originally issued on Chicago-based Vee-Jay Records, which was owned by a black couple, Vivian and James Bracken, and their cousin Calvin Carter. Before going out of business in 1965, the company recorded a variety of acts, from the white harmony group the Four Seasons to the rich, thick harmonies of the Dells to rocking blues innovator John Lee Hooker. The album Vee-Jay issued was half Lennon and McCartney originals and half covers of songs originally recorded by black singers, including the Isley Brothers' "Twist and Shout" and two songs cut by the female vocal trio the Shirelles ("Baby It's You," "Boys").

The conventional wisdom is that Lennon was the rawer, more bluesy composer and McCartney the softer, more tuneful writer. Although the Beatles' catalog actually paints a more complicated picture, McCartney's now lengthy post-Beatles résumé is a lot closer to that of Holland-Dozier-Holland than to Muddy Waters's. "Silly Love Songs," McCartney's whimsical 1976 statement of artistic purpose about the value of feel-good, sing-along songwriting, is a direct antecedent of "The Girl Is Mine" and several other collaborations the ex-Beatle made, not just with Jackson, but also with another black music giant, Stevie Wonder. Between 1979 and 1984, McCartney wrote, co-wrote, and/or performed "Girlfriend," "Ebony and Ivory," "Say Say Say," and "The Girl Is Mine." To suggest that these songs are not the artistic high points for any of the three men involved is being kind.

But before we get into the merits (or lack of same) for this quartet of tunes, let's contemplate why they exist at all. During the Beatles years, McCartney collaborated primarily with Lennon, but less so as McCartney and the band splintered. After he left the Beatles, McCartney did a lot of music as a one-man band before starting Wings, which was primarily a vehicle for his songs. At one point he loosened up the reins in Wings and let other band members contribute, but that didn't last. Basically, after Lennon, McCartney didn't treat too many people as creative equals (except for his wife, Linda, whom he gave a lot more creative latitude than she deserved).

Yet ten years or so after the breakup of the Beatles, Mc-Cartney chose to collaborate with two black stars. The hookup with Wonder made perfect sense. After the Beatles broke up in 1971, Wonder became the dominant singer-songwriter in pop, with a string of landmark albums that sold millions, won Grammys, and spawned a slew of classic songs. *Talking Book* in 1972, *Innervisions* in 1973, *Fullfillingness' First Finale* in 1974, and *Songs in the Key of Life* in 1976 are some of the greatest pop recordings ever made. There was also a long-running personal relationship between the two men. In 1974 Wonder participated in a jam session in Los Angeles with Lennon and McCartney, the only reported post-Beatles musical meeting of the estranged bandmates. That they were both there demonstrated the respect they held for Wonder.

As great as Wonder and McCartney can be, both men have a real sweet tooth when it comes to the syrupy, heavy-handed imagery and cutesy melodies ("You Are the Sunshine of My Life," "Michelle") from which "Ebony and Ivory" suffers. There is a nice contrast in the melody between minor keys in the opening verses and the majors of the hook, and, of course, a plea for racial harmony can't be faulted. Yet there is something unforgivingly perky about the last section of the song that trivializes a serious subject. "Ebony and Ivory" was a massive hit at the time of its release in 1982, but the song hasn't worn well.

Thankfully, Quincy's taste for quality material was at work in the selection of McCartney's "Girlfriend" for *Off the Wall.*

In acting as an intermediary between the ex-Beatle and Michael, Quincy found a song with several clever melody lines that played to Michael's natural boyishness, while also bringing out his soulful side in the song's last section. "Girlfriend" is also a nice contrast to Wonder's contribution to the album, "I Can't Help It," a song about being sucked into a passionate love affair. If "Girlfriend" is about a teen becoming a man, "I Can't Help It" is about a young man encountering his first serious love, a nice bookend that adds dimension and complexity to *Off the Wall* as a listening experience.

After *Off the Wall*, McCartney and Michael finally met and bonded. They went on to collaborate on several songs, the most prominent of which were "Say Say Say," written by McCartney and produced by George Martin, who had helmed all the Beatles' classic recordings, and "The Girl Is Mine," which Michael wrote and Quincy produced. In a sense both songs were sequels to "Ebony and Ivory" because they both paired one of the world's biggest 1960s pop stars with a black star, whom the Beatle treated as an equal, an idea that was almost radical in the segregated world of pop. The video for "Say Say Say," an elaborate production that depicted the two stars as carnival performers, and the lyric for "The Girl Is Mine," with the two verbally wrestling over a girl, were explicit antiracist statements well worth making at the start of the Reagan era. "The Girl," the first single off *Thriller* and released in October 1982, was a pop hit, but it was met with lots of grumbling by African Americans unimpressed by the song's perceived advocacy of interracial dating and its apparent retreat from *Off the Wall*'s great dance music.

Ultimately, the most significant aspect of the collaborations between Paul McCartney and Michael Jackson had nothing to do with the music the two made together. Though Michael had been around Berry Gordy and other smart music businessmen for years, it was a casual conversation with McCartney that inspired Michael to investigate music publishing as a source of revenue, foreshadowing a business deal that would be the most important of Michael's life.

A LITTLE BEATLES BACKSTORY is necessary here. In 1963, McCartney, Lennon, and their manager, Brian Epstein, sold their publishing rights to Northern Songs to avoid paying a huge percentage of their incomes in British taxes. They would continue to receive their songwriting royalties directly, but their publishing royalties (the other 50 percent) would be filtered through the tax shelter of Northern Songs.

This antitax strategy worked well for six years until famous businessman Lord Lew Grade mounted a takeover bid for Northern Songs, which succeeded in large part because McCartney and Lennon couldn't agree on how to rebuff Grade's efforts. On one level this was great for the Beatles because Grade's aggressive campaign raised the stock's worth to almost seven times its original value. On another level it irked these two incredibly successful men that they could not control all aspects of their classic catalog.

Michael entered the picture in 1985 when the Beatles' publishing, by then part of the 4,000-plus songs in the ATV Music catalog, was put on the market. Of that number, only about 200 of the songs belonged to the Beatles. Apparently, McCartney was seeking to grab just the Beatles' songs when Michael scooped up ATV for $47.5 million. Obviously, this shrewd and aggressive business move did little for Michael and McCartney's relationship.

With the ATV catalog (which also included songs from Buddy Holly and Sly Stone) generating income from films, movies, and commercials, the songs became Michael's financial backbone for the rest of his life. Beatles purists worried that Michael would license Beatles songs for cheesy TV ads (a fear that was borne out when "Revolution" was sold for use in a 1987 Nike commercial). But, overall, he was respectful of the music, and the music was good to him. In 1995, he got $95 million from Sony for half of his ATV holdings, and a few years before his death, the ATV songs were used as collateral to secure a $270 million loan from Bank of America. It's a weird irony that Michael financed the lavish lifestyle of his last years, in large part, with revenues generated from songs created by R&B fans Lennon and McCartney.

" T H R I L L E R "

T HERE ARE SO MANY ASPECTS TO "THRILLER," the most important communal dance of the last three decades, that it's hard to know where to start. But the root of the story is not Rod Temperton, who wrote the tune to Quincy's specifications, or Michael, whose interest in horror films inspired the vision, or even John Landis, the clever Hollywood director who directed the video. The root is Michael Peters, who died of AIDS in Los Angeles in 1994, way too soon to have seen his choreography danced around the world.

Born in Williamsburg, Brooklyn, to a black father and a Jewish mother, Peters was a product of the vibrant New York dance culture of the 1970s. He performed with legendary black companies such as Alvin Ailey and Talley Beatty while dancing on the weekends at the city's many gay and black discos. Broadway was slowly beginning to open up to black dancers in white shows and black musicals in general, and there was a new sense of possibility among dancers and choreographers.

There are early examples of Peters's work on sexpot dancer/singer Lola Falana's mid-1970s television specials (which were reissued on DVD in 2009). Peters can be seen next to the lithe Falana, using some of the hip movements and leg lifts that would appear in "Beat It" a few years later. Peters got his first major break as a choreographer working on a video for Donna Summer's erotic epic "Love to Love You Baby," though that work was seen primarily in Europe, where music videos had been long established. In 1979 he got to work on a Broadway show called *Comin' Uptown,* a black interpretation of Charles Dickens's *A Christmas Carol* that starred superb actor and tap dancer Gregory Hines.

What really put Peters on the map was his work as co-choreographer of *Dreamgirls,* the faux Motown musical masterminded by director/writer Michael Bennett. The show, which was Bennett's follow-up to the classic backstage musical *A Chorus Line,* rewrote the Motown success as a love triangle. The Berry Gordy–like label head tosses aside an Aretha Franklin–styled soul shouter for a slender Diana Ross–inspired pop diva. Though the musical's fictitious story line rankled Motown loyalists, the production's innovative staging and choreography, a blend of classic R&B stagecraft with Broadway theatricality, made the show a smash.

The rave reviews for *Dreamgirls* are undoubtedly what landed Peters on Michael's radar screen. "Beat It," the video of which was basically a West Coast *West Side Story* set among Bloods and Crips, features Peters as one of the gang leaders. (The other gang leader, played by Vincent Patterson, would go on to choreograph "Smooth Criminal" and other Jackson videos.)

In retrospect, there's not much actual dancing in "Beat It." Michael flashes some quick moves on his nocturnal journey to the gang fight, but the big ensemble moves that symbolize Michael's reconciling the two warring groups are only in the video's last minute. Nevertheless, what was there was striking enough to make Peters a star in the burgeoning new field of music video choreography, where he'd do particularly memorable work on Pat Benatar's "Love Is a Battlefield," giving the gangly rock diva some new wave dance moves that worked despite her lack of rhythm.

But Peters's entry into dance history was assured by the dancing zombies of "Thriller." He took the stiff-legged, lurching walk of scores of zombie movies, particularly George A. Romero's cult classic *Dawn of the Dead,* and created hunched-back turns, creepy head jerks, and slide steps graceful in their clunkiness. Campy by definition, Peters's dance was silly fun that transcended generations and national boundaries, and, crucially, it was danceable by regular folks without any dance training or skills. In many ways, this dance is Michael Jackson's most perfect pop product. It was good, pseudocreepy, dress-up fun that even folks in countries without a Halloween tradition could get into.

AT THE TIME OF PETERS'S DEATH, rebel cultures, hip–hop, and grunge dominated popular culture, with West Coast gangsters and angst-ridden rockers in flannel shirts all the rage. The blend of big Broadway gestures and modern dance Peters specialized in was not in vogue, having been supplanted in videos by slam dancing and new forms of street dance. That Michael's reputation was deeply scarred by a child abuse scandal in 1994 made the "Thriller" dance seem even more passé.

But by the middle of the twenty-first century's first decade, 1980s nostalgia was rampant in music, fashion, and design as the children of MTV, John Hughes, and Ronald Regan came of age. This retro aesthetic brought "Thriller" back in ways planned and playfully unexpected. In February 2008, to celebrate the twenty-fifth anniversary of *Thriller*'s release, Sony records had flash mobs break into the dance in public spaces around the world. It was a canny piece of marketing by the multinational corporation, but a pale copy of a gloriously crazy Filipino prisoner video. Posted on YouTube by Byron F. Garcia, the warden of a maximum-security prison in Cebu, Philippines, the clip captures 1,500 male inmates dressed in orange jumpsuits (and a few in nontheatrical chains) doing Peters's dance in the prison courtyard.

As a form of exercise and tension release among the prisoners, Garcia had been using elaborate dance performances for a while, with communal (and decidedly gay-friendly) tracks such as the Village People's "Y.M.C.A." and "In the Navy" in the mix. One of the elements that made the Cebu dance so popular was that Wenjiel Resane, an openly gay ex-pizza chef, played Ola Ray in a halter top and tight jeans with an appropriately frightened expression. At the time of this writing, the video had been watched by tens of millions and counting.

But my favorite manifestation of the "Thriller" dance circa the twenty-first century has its roots in Kitchener, Ontario, in 1997. There, sixteen-year-old Ines Markeljevic, who as a child had been fascinated by the video, was now studying dance. She convinced a teacher to show her the steps to "Thriller," which at the time was being performed at Halloween parties.

Jump forward to Toronto circa 2006, where Markeljevic, by now earning a living as a Pilates teacher and dance instructor, organized sixty-two dancers to perform the dance. Inspired by the response, and with a nice feel for the pulse of global culture, she organized "Thrill the World." Harnessing the Internet's ability to coordinate masses of people for a single cause, she got groups of dancers around the world to do the dance at the same time.

Following Michael's passing, "Thrill the World," which had already caught on, was performed by more than 4,000 dancers in seventy-one cities—from Matlock, England, to Selma, California, to Austin, Texas, to Philadelphia, Pennsylvania. Some of the groups had only eight people. Others numbered in the hundreds. Some folks had on elaborate costumes, and others dabbed on a bit of makeup and got into some scruffy clothes.

On YouTube one afternoon I sat and watched the "Thrill the World" folks dance to Peters's steps, emulate Michael's moves, and dress up like zombies from 1984. On one level this event was as hokey as it gets. But I felt the pathos as schoolteachers and businessmen, the serious and the silly, the graceful and the gawky, jerked around like movie monsters for fun and the memory of Michael. Indeed, this event was Michael Jackson's perfect pop moment—we are the world with a pelvic thrust.

" B E A T   I T "

I N THE 1940S, CARL HOGAN WAS THE ORIGINAL
guitarist in the Tympany Five, a driving, jukebox-rocking
band led by Louis Jordan, one of the leading black pop
stars of the World War II era. From 1938 to 1946, Jordan's
peak years, he enjoyed hits such as "Ain't Nobody Here but
Us Chickens," "Caldonia," and "Five Guys Named Moe." "I
made just as much money off white people as I did colored,"
he reflected years later. "I could play a white joint this week
and a colored next."

Jordan was a broad-smiling, funny-as-hell saxophonist/
singer who fused scaled-back big horn arrangements, a
smoking rhythm section that specialized in rabbit-quick shuf-
fles, and delightful story songs into a string of hits that would
be labeled rhythm and blues (in 1947 by *Billboard* columnist,
and future record producer, Jerry Wexler) and rock and roll.

Initially, people called Jordan's music "jump blues," a reflection of the music's up-tempo energy and bluesy roots.

On "Ain't That Just Like a Woman (They'll Do It Every Time)" (in 1946) and other Jordan tracks, Hogan, using the still relatively new electric guitar, played intros, fills, and solos that simplified Charlie Christian's jazz chops, while being a lot more playful in tone than the hard-core blues guitarist would have been at the time. Under the canny commercial guidance of Jordan and producer Milt Gabler, Hogan's play created a link among an African American musical star, the electric guitar, and crossover appeal that would peak with *Thriller* some forty years later.

There's another important connection between Jordan in the 1940s and Jackson in the 1980s, and it's visual. Because Jordan was a dynamic performer, he, with the aid of Gabler, produced a series of "soundies," aka music videos, that were screened on jukeboxes that could show short films and that were shown as shorts prior to feature films at theaters catering to black audiences. Jordan wasn't a dancer, but he had remarkable charisma and vitality, which popped on the screen.

IT WAS JORDAN'S PRODUCER, Milt Gabler, who supervised the recording of Bill Haley's "Rock Around the Clock" in 1954, which employed a simplified "big beat" rhythm under an arrangement that otherwise echoed Jordan's hits. Although Haley was a one-hit wonder, the idea of a Jordan feel driven by an electric bass, trap drums playing in 4/4 time, and, for energy and flavor, a loud electric guitar was picked up and refined by Jordan's inheritor, Chuck Berry. Aside from Jordan's obvious influence on Berry's singing style and storytelling lyrics, Hogan was the most important influence on Berry's own dynamic guitar picking.

With Hogan's lithe style hovering in the distant background, Berry made a Negro playing a guitar like he was ringing a bell as much a part of rock and roll as a pair of blue suede shoes. Although Bo Diddley, Ike Turner, and T-Bone Walker were among the many other sepia-toned guitar heroes of the Eisenhower era, Berry led the way. He duck-walked into teenage hearts from 1955 to 1959, alongside Elvis, Fats Domino, Jerry Lee Lewis, and other rock and roll wild men.

Then, in late 1959, Berry was prosecuted under the Mann Act and charged with statutory rape for traveling across state lines with a fourteen-year-old Spanish-speaking Apache girl. Reputedly, she was a prostitute, but Berry hired her as a hatcheck girl at his St. Louis nightclub. He subsequently fired her, and the young lady, bitter at her dismissal, went to the local police. Berry was arrested and, after two trials, sentenced to two years in a federal penitentiary in Indiana. In a harbinger of Jackson's career, the sex scandal effectively ended Berry's and left him with a bitterness that he still carries.

After his release in 1964, Berry performed relentlessly, never traveling with a band, always using local musicians (after all, everyone knew his songs), and demanding to be paid in cash before taking the stage. Aside from a 1972 novelty hit with the risqué "My Ding-a-Ling," Berry never had another hit.

The culture (and the marketplace) had changed. The nomenclature had shifted from rock and roll to rock, from rhythm and blues to soul. Three-minute records had given way to three-minute guitar solos, mostly played by white British guitar players. Throughout most of the 1960s, young black men who rocked didn't become stars (though old black blues men such as B. B. King and Muddy Waters did pick up white rock fans).

THE EXCEPTION THAT PROVED the rule was James Marshall "Jimi" Hendrix (born Johnny Allen Hendrix). In 1965, he was a charismatic R&B backup guitarist playing clubs in Harlem behind soul belters Percy Sledge and Wilson Pickett, his hair processed and wearing a tux. A year later he was living in London, having reinvented himself as a psychedelic rock star with two white side men and multicolored outfits, with an Afro soon to come. The showmanship that so enthralled, and intimidated, so many in the segregated rock world was Hendrix employing the tricks he'd learned playing on the chitlin' circuit.

As a performer, Hendrix, like Jackson years later, placed the lessons of flamboyance he had learned in black show business in front of white audiences. That both were eccentric geniuses made these crossover moves seem less like calculations and more like projections of their rich fantasy lives. Hendrix dreamed of castles made of sand; Jackson imagined Hollywood noirs in which he was the blessed redeemer.

Where Berry had been one of the major black faces of rock and roll, Hendrix was the only true black rock star of the 1960s (I'm not counting Sly Stone here, who was a pop star more than a rocker). For all the peace and love pronouncements, 1960s white rock culture existed in a world as musically segregated as the South its young people vilified. Fans knew the songs of Berry, mostly through covers by the Beatles, the Beach Boys, the Grateful Dead, and others, but black rockers save Hendrix got no love. And if he hadn't moved to Europe (like so many other black artists before him), he might not have broken through in America.

After Hendrix's drug-related accidental death in 1970 (the same year the Jackson 5 conquered the charts), rock radio, which had been a relatively free-form format, became codified as AOR (album-oriented rock), a tightly formatted approach to programming that certified certain tracks as classics (Hendrix's "Purple Haze," "All Along the Watchtower," "Hey Joe," and "Foxy Lady" are among the songs that made the cut) and allowed in rock acts that played guitar-dominated music. The casual musical segregation of the 1960s was cemented by radio programmers and consultants in the 1970s. The idea that black bands didn't play rock became a self-fulfilling prophecy because record labels were reluctant to sign black rockers. Truly freaky black rockers such as Funkadelic had to play funk as Parliament to make ends meet.

Prince, who made true rock guitar–based songs (along with several other styles), was flatly rejected by AOR during his first five albums. I interviewed the program director of New York's rock powerhouse WNEW-FM in 1981, and he told me with no hesitation that he'd never play Prince on his station. Opening for the Rolling Stones at RFK Stadium in Philadelphia that same year, the singer-songwriter was cursed by fans and had beer bottles hurled in his direction. Despite his brilliance, Prince joined lesser-known acts, such as the integrated Mother's Finest and Betty Davis, which couldn't build a white rock constituency. If you heard a non-Hendrix black voice on rock radio in the 1980s, it was Rolling Stones backup singer Merry Clayton wailing away at the end of "Gimme Shelter."

Black radio wasn't any more open-minded. Radio stations might play Earth, Wind and Fire's cover of the Beatles' "Got to Get You into My Life," with its tasteful guitar, but little else that smacked of rock. Ernie Isley, drummer and guitarist of the Isley Brothers, apparently had a special rock pass that allowed him to play Hendrix-inspired solos on records like "Who's That Lady." But the guitars were mixed so that the tone was rather thin and not as commanding as it sounded at the Isleys' live show.

IT IS AGAINST THIS HISTORY of African Americans and rock guitar that Jackson and Quincy created "Beat It." Apparently, Quincy was the instigator of the song, inspired by the Knack's hokey 1979 hit, "My Sharona." This is an odd reference point: The Knack was a one-album wonder roundly disliked by most rock critics, and the era abounded with countless other pop rock hits from which to draw.

But rock wasn't exactly Quincy's specialty; in his extensive body of work as a producer up to 1983, there's nary a rock track in the bunch. Rock was definitely new terrain for the vet. But his commercial instinct that a well-executed rock record would open *Thriller* up to a wider, whiter pop audience was right on. Surprisingly, the demo of "Beat It," released on the *This Is It* compilation, isn't very rock oriented. There are no guitars or much else on the demo other than Michael's vocal brilliance, as we hear him stacking harmonies for the backing vocals with his usual diligence.

The intro to "Beat It" is actually a little misleading. When the jarring Synclavier kicks it over a stiff-sounding drum machine beat, it sounds as if Jackson is about to reference the underground electro-funk sound coming out of New York. A great many people think Eddie Van Halen played guitar on the entire record. In truth, the fat, aggressive sound that gave "Beat It" its personality was played by Toto's Steve Lukather and David Williams, with Lukather getting an arranging credit for his work on the track. Lukather, who'd played lead guitar on Toto's hits and those of many other stars, could have easily played the lead on "Beat It" and done the job.

Despite his musicianship, Lukather wasn't a badass, Jack Daniels–swilling, rock guitar god like Eddie Van Halen. It was Van Halen who gave hard-rock credibility to an artist who, for all his talent, was seen as a soft-spoken R&B/dance act, just the kind of performer rock radio was designed not to play. Though the magnificent music video for "Beat It" was certainly crucial, the record probably wouldn't have meant as much when it was released if Van Halen hadn't played the solo on it.

As a young music critic at *Billboard,* I reviewed Van Halen's first headlining show in New York, a gig at the steamy rock venue the Palladium, on East 14th Street. Lead singer David Lee Roth, with his long, swinging hair, athletic body, and splits, was the visual center of the band and was crucial to its MTV appeal. But Eddie's quicksilver fingers and inventive solos created sonic textures that were both fun and very personal. In an era when rock solos were at an indulgent peak, Eddie Van Halen's work announced that there was a major new talent on the scene.

THE TALE OF EDDIE VAN HALEN'S involvement with "Beat It" starts with a funny tale of miscommunication from the era before cell phones. "The phone in my house wasn't working too well," the guitar legend told *Musician* magazine in 1984. "I could tell the person on the other end of the line couldn't hear me. Quincy called and asked 'Eddie?' I say 'Who's this?' He didn't say anything 'cause he couldn't hear me. So I hung up. He called back. Same thing—he couldn't hear me. Third time he calls back, he goes 'Eddie?' And I said, 'What the fuck you want you asshole?' He says 'This is Quincy. Quincy Jones.' 'Oh my God. I'm sorry. I'm sorry. I get so many crank calls that I didn't know.'"

Once that comic confusion was straightened out, Van Halen had his regular engineer, Donn Landee, pick up the tape of "Beat It" from Westlake and bring it over to his house. After a listen, Van Halen asked for some changes, primarily over which part of the track he'd solo. He spoke with Quincy, and the alterations were made. On the day he recorded his historic solo, Quincy and Jackson stood behind Eddie as he made two passes at a guitar part that has become an air guitar classic.

At the time Van Halen cut that solo, he wasn't paid for it. "I didn't care," he told *Musician* magazine in 1984. "I did it as a favor. I didn't want nothing. . . . Maybe Michael will give me dance lessons someday. . . . People don't understand that. I was [a] complete fool, according to the rest of the band and our manager and everybody else." Just as Michael was given rock cred by Eddie Van Halen, the performance on "Beat It" helped Van Halen become a bigger pop group, with the band's single "Jump" making the black singles' chart and receiving black radio play. "I'm obsessed with music," Van Halen said, "and I get off on playing and I don't care how much money someone makes off it. Put it this way: I was not used. I knew what I was doing. I don't do anything unless I want to do it."

Despite the success of "Beat It" for Jackson, the song did not open the floodgates for black rock. But I do believe the acceptance of "Beat It" in particular, and *Thriller* overall, made it easier for America to accept Prince, an androgynous cult figure, as a pop star. He had been making rock records way before the 1984 *Purple Rain* album (such as "Bambi," from *Prince* in 1979, and "When You Were Mine," from *Dirty Mind* in 1981). And each of Prince's pre–*Purple Rain* albums (*Dirty Mind, Controversy, 1999*) sold more than 1 million copies and the supporting tour for each had hit larger venues. But *Thriller* showed Prince's label (Warner Bros.), the retail community, and radio programmers the growing possibilities of a young black pop performer.

Of course, the movie *Purple Rain* worked for Prince in the same way videos did for Jackson, giving a modern visual dimension to his music. The funny thing about Prince, given his considerable charisma and good looks, was that pre–*Purple Rain* he'd never really made any great videos. Most of his clips had been multicamera re-creations of his live show, which *Purple Rain* was, too. It was definitely a reflection of Prince's otherworldly confidence that, in an era of increasingly conceptual videos, his visual expressions were all about capturing his band and himself.

IN THE YEARS AFTER "BEAT IT" and "Purple Rain," a number of R&B acts tried to use rock guitars as a route to larger sales (Shalamar's "Dead Giveaway," Cameo's "Candy," Janet

Jackson's "Black Cat"). The black group that was most successful in fusing rock with its musical approach came from
well outside the mainstream. Run-D.M.C., the self-
proclaimed king of rock, whether produced by Larry Smith
and Russell Simmons or by Simmons with Rick Rubin, made
rap rock records that were credible to both black street kids
and suburban rock fans. And Run's collaboration with Aerosmith on "Walk This Way" was the son of "Beat It" and just as
culturally influential. Out of Run-D.M.C's rap rock came
Public Enemy's wall of samples, eventually inspiring a whole
rap rock genre of bands incendiary (Rage Against the Machine) and insipid (Limp Bizkit).

Yet aside from Prince and the Revolution, no actual black
bands made the rock pantheon. The closest was Living
Colour, the flagship band of the Black Rock Coalition, a collective of New York–based critics, activists, and musicians
whose avowed mission was to reconnect black music to the
rocking tradition that Berry and Hendrix represented.
Backed with an endorsement from Mick Jagger (who produced the tracks "Glamour Boys" and "Which Way to America?" on its 1988 album, *Vivid*), Living Colour crashed the
MTV color line with the anthemic "Cult of Personality." To
see Vernon Reid, a product of New York's avant-garde jazz
circles, shredding on his multicolored guitar in between
videos by Madonna and Guns and Roses was truly exciting.

After the band opened for the Rolling Stones on a stadium
tour and made two successful albums, the band's third release, *Stain,* fell flat. That it contained a song called "Elvis Is

Dead," criticizing rock and roll's great white father, may or may not have something to do with the album's reception, but Living Colour never became the consistent commercial/artist force I, along with many other early fans, had hoped.

ONE EXAMPLE OF THE enduring appeal of "Beat It" can be found in Fall Out Boy, a twenty-first-century pop-rock band. This staple on MTV when MTV actually focused on videos went from performing "Beat It" on stage to recording it and doing an elaborate video homage full of bejeweled gloves, red jackets, and *Thriller*-era visual signifiers.

After Prince, Run-D.M.C., and Living Colour, the act most affected by the song's success was Michael Jackson himself. For the rest of his career, Michael would regularly record wannabe rock anthems, often in collaborations with other rock guitar gods (Slash of Guns and Roses played on "Dirty Diana") or in duets (the contrived, terrible "State of Shock" with Mick Jagger; the vibrant, playful "Scream" with sister Janet). But none of his subsequent efforts were as vital or as important as "Beat It," which remains the most important black rock record in the years since Jimi Hendrix's death.

"BILLIE JEAN"

OVER THE YEARS, MICHAEL WOULD TELL A couple of versions of the story about the girl who inspired his greatest song, but in a sense the particulars don't matter. Originally titled "Not My Lover," the lyric encapsulated years of fear of women, from girls tearing at his clothes when he was a kid, to his brothers having raw sex with groupies, to his being aggressively pursued by women throughout his young adulthood. The theme of the devouring, man-eating woman is as old in American song as the blues, as essential to rock as the electric guitar, and lives on with misogynistic gusto in hip-hop's DNA. Men with too easy access to sex often become satyrs who revile the women they bed even as they feast on the bounty. Michael, unlike his brothers, never indulged, but good Virgo that he was, he observed and remembered it all.

By 1982 Michael had gone out with Tatum O'Neal and Brooke Shields and counted Diana Ross, Liza Minnelli, and other show biz divas as confidantes. Whatever he'd already personally experienced with women, whatever he'd been advised by the older women in his life, "Billie Jean" suggested that his understanding of the opposite sex was very much a work in progress. And maybe that's one reason it works: In defining "Billie Jean," he actually revealed his own insecurity and wariness of sex, opposite and otherwise.

"Billie Jean" is one of those rare recordings whose greatness is apparent the first time you hear it, and as with so many things Michael Jackson, it starts with the rhythm. The pelvic thrusting, the sharp angular lines of Jackson's body, and that black fedora held tightly on his head all flow from that profound introductory beat, which has been emulated, referenced, and plain old stolen on countless pop songs since 1983.

The song's rock solid, yet sweetly shuffling beat is the consummation of marrying technology to a studio-skilled drummer. The basic rhythm was recorded by Michael on a drum machine at his home in Encino, and that drum machine beat remained the core of the record for most of the *Thriller* sessions until, in the hectic final weeks of finishing the record, Jackson and Quincy rethought the "Billie Jean" beat.

Top session drummer Ndugu Chancler was called in to the Westwood studio to enhance that rhythm. "I was placed in a room by myself, so there was no leakage," Chancler told me in 1984. "Both Quincy and Michael came in to suggest things for the two or three hours it took to cut the track. I played it through about eight to ten times." This combination of drum machine and Chancler, playing a nine-piece jacaranda wood drum set, was merged by engineer Bruce Swedien.

At the prodding of Jones, who asserted that "this piece of music has to have the most unique sonic personality of anything that we have ever recorded," Swedien brought in a special kick drum cover made with a slot in the front where a mic could be slipped in and then zipped up tight against the drum skin. Swedien had fellow engineer George Massenburg, who was responsible for the incredibly crisp drum sounds on Earth, Wind and Fire's records, bring over a portable twelve-channel mixing console just to capture the rhythm section, isolating those sounds from the rest of the track.

Hand in hand with that drumbeat is the song's vibrant bass line. "Michael was very specific about how he wanted the bass line to sound," recalled bassist Louis Johnson. "He had me bring all my guitars to see how they sounded playing the part. I tried three or four basses before we settled on the Yamaha. It's really live with a lot of power and guts. If you'd have heard me on a different bass on 'Billie Jean,' you'd have said, 'Use the Yamaha.' On the basic riff I overdubbed three parts to strengthen its power." Later, keyboardist Greg Phillinganes would overdub and deepen the bass line on "Billie Jean" (and most other tracks on *Thriller*).

Veteran Jerry Hey arranged the strings that heightened the record's tension. "If you listen to the strings only, you'll swear you're in Carnegie Hall," claimed engineer Swedien.

"It has a very natural stereo spread. The recording of it is as legitimate and straight forward as a classical recording."

The balance of Michael's urgent lead vocal and his backing arrangements is the record's emotional core. It could be argued that in later years Michael's vocal embellishments were too often just that, embellishments, not details that heightened the lyric's message and tightened the song's groove. But on "Billie Jean" all his asides and flourishes are so well placed that they sound like wordless pleas for help, conveying exasperation and discomfort, fear and frustration. Yet they are always in the song's pocket, driving the track into the realm of pop anthem even while exorcising a very personal demon. Part of the magic of the supporting harmonies is that many of them were sung through a mail tube, adding a sense of distance. But that passionate lead vocal was recorded in one hot-blooded take.

Quincy was very proud to later tell reporters about having had saxophonist Tom Scott come in late in the production process to "sweeten" the track with a Lyricon, a high-pitched wind instrument. "It was Quincy's idea to weave this little thread into the thing," Swedien said. "It was a last-minute overdub thing. Quincy calls it 'ear candy.' You're not conscious of it. It's just a subliminal element that works."

I have listened to "Billie Jean" a zillion times and have never heard Scott's playing, but then that is the point. The attention to detail, too small to be heard but nevertheless quietly felt, is just one of the many reasons that this recording was a true work of pop art even before Michael moonwalked.

"HUMAN NATURE"

O N THE LIST OF PERFORMERS AT THE MICHAEL
Jackson memorial at the Staples Arena, the most
surprising name was that of John Mayer. Unlike
Smokey Robinson, Stevie Wonder, or Lionel Richie, who
were Motown comrades, or Usher, who was profoundly influenced by Michael, Mayer was a white guitarist/singer who
didn't make his first recordings until the twenty-first century.
He'd tried his hand at some soulful-sounding records and had
recorded some blues standards, but he had no real direct connection to Michael. In fact, the two men had never met. But
like every young person of his generation, Mayer had grown
up with Michael's music. To a great extent for a musician of
Mayer's age (he was born in 1977), a lot of his ideas about
what a pop song was (and wasn't) had come via *Thriller.*

The Jackson family reached out and asked Mayer to perform "Human Nature," and he wrestled for two days with

how to do the song. Finally, he decided not to sing (figuring he didn't have the chops for that), but instead opted to play the melody on guitar. Mayer's instrumental version of "Human Nature" was wistful and sweet, despite his tendency to make unflattering facial expressions while playing.

WHETHER INTENTIONAL OR NOT, the choice of Mayer to play "Human Nature" worked as a nod to the white pop craftsmen who had been central to the song's creation. Mayer, a maker of mass appeal mainstream pop ("Your Body Is a Wonderland"), is one of the few twenty-first-century stars whose hits echo the heyday of LA studio perfectionism. Toto, a group of LA session aces turned pop band, were not just symbols of that style but also played a central musical role in the making of *Thriller*. Composed of guitarist Steve Lukather, keyboardist David Paich, bassist David Hungate, drummer Jeff Porcaro, and his brother Steve on keys, they all grew up in North Hollywood and most attended the same high school, where they began their careers as a band called Rural Still Life.

Well trained and very collaborative, the members of this crew built a rep around LA as session axmen able to please picky studio perfectionists such as Steely Dan's demanding Walter Becker and Donald Fagen. Their skill was apparent on Toto's self-titled 1977 debut, which spawned the pop-rock hit "Hold the Line" and sold more than 1 million copies. For many critics, it also made them symbols of a slick, glib sound that disgusted the angry apostles of punk rock in New York, London, and elsewhere. Along with Journey, Chicago, and several other one-named white bread bands of the 1970s, rock critics seriously disliked Toto.

But in the cloistered world of LA pop, Toto was royalty with a nice appreciation for R&B. "Georgy Porgy," a single on the first album featuring black singer Cheryl Lynn, received considerable play on black radio and led the strong-voiced vocalist to land a record deal. Toto's 1982 album, *Toto IV*, contained the Grammy song of the year, "Rosanna," and was named album of the year.

Just the year before, Quincy's album *The Dude* had won that honor, so when he recruited members of Toto to play on *Thriller*, he was bringing in musicians who knew a great deal about making commercial records. They played a number of important roles on *Thriller*, with Steve Lukather in a particularly key role because he arranged and played most of the guitars on "Beat It." Not surprising, considering Toto's success, Quincy also asked the band to submit some songs.

The oft-told tale is that Paich put some songs on a cassette for Quincy, but they didn't interest him. The tape kept playing in Quincy's office, and at the end of the tape was a rough demo of a song from Steve Porcaro. Quincy has said the fragment contained the famous "Why, why, why" section. In the delicacy and jazzy feel of the melody, Quincy, as good a judge of a pop song as anybody in the 1980s, heard a vehicle for Michael and an element that was missing from the album.

Quincy pulled out of his Rolodex the number of lyricist

John Bettis, a songwriter with a knack for penning graceful pop sentiments with a hint of sex. He worked on the Carpenters' "Yesterday Once More." He wrote the Pointer Sisters' "Slow Hand" and Madonna's first successful pop ballad, "Crazy for You." Bettis, who also had a long list of TV and movie theme credits, was a craftsman who, in the course of two days, pulled together Porcaro's melody with beguiling words contoured to Michael's persona.

Appropriately, "Human Nature" engenders Michael's quietest vocal on *Thriller*. He's slightly breathy at the start and then softly urgent the rest of the way, building to the "Why, why, why" section that caps the performance. On the key line, "If this town is just an apple, let me take a bite," Michael has just the right tone of boyish yearning. Around Michael's voice Lukather arranged little murmuring guitar riffs to support the song's ethereal mood.

In 1981 on *The Man with the Horn*, trumpet maestro Miles Davis, like Quincy one of the few bebop era figures relevant in the age of the synthesizer, covered "Human Nature." It's a tribute to Porcaro's melody and the structure Bettis brought to it that this song beguiled the ears of Quincy Jones, Michael Jackson, and Miles Davis. (It would also have a very active hip-hop life as a sample.) So Mayer's decision to do an instrumental version at the tribute was quite apt. Though written by two Hollywood pros, not Michael, "Human Nature" is one of the most recognizable melodies associated with the singer and absolutely the best one on *Thriller*.

"PYT
(PRETTY YOUNG
THING)"

I N THE CONTEXT OF THE TITANIC SALES OF *THRILLER*, Quincy Jones's own artistic journey is often forgotten. Quincy was hardly idle between recording with Michael. In fact, Quincy's 1981 album, *The Dude*, sold more than 1 million copies and won five Grammys, including album of the year. The songs on that album reflected his continued development as a pop music producer, while contributing to his track record as a talent scout.

The Dude was anchored by the performance of the deep-voiced James Ingram, who sonically would have been right at home wailing on a Stax single backed by Booker T. and the MGs. But this record was made in 1980, a time when crossover to white audiences drove most creative decisions for black singers. The son of a deacon and the product of a very religious family, Ingram, like any true soul singer, was charmed by secular songs. He played in a funk band called Revelation Funk, on vocals and keyboards, which eventually took him to Los Angeles. There Ingram's musical skills landed him gigs as a backup vocalist for Ray Charles and session work for Marvin Gaye.

In the musical hot pot of 1970s Los Angeles, Quincy heard about Ingram via his demo for a big ballad called "Just Once," a tune written by a team of songwriters. After hearing Ingram's ballad, Quincy cannily chose two Ingram ballad performances to launch both the singer's career and Quincy's next studio album, *The Dude*. "Just Once" was the slow-building saga of a couple trying to keep a fragile union together. Ingram sang the song with restrained emotion, containing his vocals within the melody, so that his soul could be felt even without being fully unleashed. "One Hundred Ways," penned by veteran songwriting team Barry Mann and Cynthia Weil, has a sweeter quality and a charming hook that reminds me of something Paul McCartney might have written on a good day.

The direction Quincy chose for Ingram—a restrained ballad performance by a natural soul singer—would be a staple of 1980s pop. The ballads Lionel Richie sang and composed for the Commodores in the late 1970s ("Easy," "Sail On") laid the groundwork for this strategy. Years before his solo success, Richie had helped the band break through to the pop charts by toning down the funk, writing great melodies, and refining his skills as a color-blind balladeer.

When you look back at Richie's records in this period, Ingram's two hits on *The Dude,* and songs such as Peaches and Herb's "Reunited" and the Manhattans' "Shining Star," you can see that they opened up a path for black singers that Richie's solo work and, later, Whitney Houston would take. As opposed to disco, which had been producer-oriented music that hid the talents of many great singers, Ingram's ballads put the emphasis on real vocal skill.

The trade-off, however, was that the restrained emotional delivery emphasized the blandness of so much of the material. "Soul music," in the sense it had been defined in the 1960s, was being relegated to nostalgia. Quincy understood the shift and in Ingram's work on *The Dude* found a singer-songwriter able to work on the fine line between emotive mainstream pop and banality. For his work on *The Dude,* Ingram would be nominated for three Grammys, including best new artist.

Ironically, *The Dude* would be Quincy's last album at long-time home A&M Records. At the time of the album's release, Quincy had already committed to forming his own label, Qwest, financed and distributed by the larger Warner Bros. Given more money and resources, Quincy expanded his production and publishing companies, signing a number of talented writers, including Ingram. On Qwest, Ingram would continue to find success in his role as a velvet-voiced balladeer with songs such as "How Do You Keep the Music

Playing" and "Baby, Come to Me," a duet with labelmate Patti Austin that went to number one in 1984 on the heels of being showcased on the soap opera *General Hospital*.

YET INGRAM'S MOST ENDURING contribution to pop was far removed from the sweet endearments of his hits. "PYT (Pretty Young Thing)" was black barbershop slang for a sexy young woman who was out of puberty but probably under twenty. It was a leering phrase employed by an older man eyeing a girl who (publicly) was just a little too young for him to step to. As a topic for a song, "PYT" was very far removed from "Just Once" and reflected more of Ingram's personality than his pop ballads did. I interviewed him a couple of times during the early 1980s and found him to be a very thoughtful, sometimes quirky guy—the kind of guy who'd have been getting a haircut and talking with his barber about a cute local girl who had ripened into a beauty.

That image also suggests just how different "PYT" would have sounded if Ingram had recorded it himself. Ingram's very rich, mature, sometimes raspy voice singing about a "pretty young thing" could have sounded sexy. It also could have sounded like he was an older dude at the club, buying bottles of champagne for nubile lovelies half his age. (This is a scene I've seen Quincy Jones live out many times in real life. So for a co-writer, this lyric is more personal than it seems.)

An older guy leering at a young girl is a staple of American music, but even so "PYT" would probably not have been a top-ten pop hit if Ingram had put it on one of his solo albums. Michael's man-child quality is what really sells the song. His boyishness takes the edge off the leer implicit in the lyric. It also helps to know that the "pretty young things" who sing background on the track are his sisters Janet and LaToya, which gives the song a playfulness and a buoyancy that elevate the proceedings nicely.

Despite composing a driving track that still sounds good at clubs to this day, Ingram never was a consistent maker of dance music. "Yah Mo B There," a 1984 religiously inspired duet with blue-eyed soul man Michael McDonald, was as close as Ingram got. He'd be part of another top-ten hit, "Secret Garden," with other "love men" Barry White, Al B. Sure, and El DeBarge, from Quincy's last studio album, *Back on the Block.* But as the 1980s progressed, Ingram never had the hit-making consistency of peers Richie, the great Luther Vandross, or even a less imposing singer such as Freddie Jackson.

When rappers began attacking R&B acts for being too smoothed out and slick, for not being too black or too strong, it was usually singers like Ingram they had in mind. In an attempt to stay relevant, he would, like Jackson, employ new jack swing creator Teddy Riley to produce a single for him. "It's Real," in 1989, was a transparent, and not very convincing, attempt to be part of the R&B/hip-hop hybrid that was redefining black music. Ingram continues to perform to this day, his voice a little rougher, but the ballads still sweet.

"PYT" WAS THE SEVENTH, and last, top-ten single from *Thriller,* and it only peaked at number ten, so it was far from the most popular single from the album during its original sales cycle. But over time, it has actually grown in popularity. The week after Jackson's death, "PYT" was the ninth most downloaded Michael Jackson song, more than "Wanna Be Startin' Somethin'," "Rock with You," and "Bad," which were all more successful back in the 1980s.

"PYT" is the most conventional-sounding song on the album. It was added late by Quincy and wasn't worried over by Michael, as so much of the material seems to have been. Even though Michael brought his personality to bear on the song, it's not as uniquely his as "Billie Jean" or even "Human Nature," songs he didn't write, though it feels as if he did.

Why the durability of "PYT"? Part of it could be exhaustion. The major dance tracks ("Billie Jean," "Wanna Be Startin' Somethin'") were played so much in the post-*Thriller* years that "PYT" eventually benefited from its own relative obscurity. If any single off *Thriller* could still sound fresh on an oldies radio station or at an old-school party, this is the record.

"LADY IN MY LIFE"

T IS OCTOBER 30, 2009, DEVIL'S NIGHT IN CANADA. In tribute to Michael Jackson, a party and a cut-for-cut performance of *Thriller* are held at the Great Hall in Toronto. Neo-soul singer Ivana Santilli, who's been asked by the promoters to sing "Lady in My Life," suddenly finds herself humping a microphone stand while performing. "I had no idea that would happen," she recalls a few weeks later. "But that song—it requires a lot of passion."

Ivana, of Toronto's surprisingly busy R&B scene and a fixture since her stellar 1999 debut, *Brown*, had been immediately intimidated at the thought of singing "Lady in My Life." "That song requires you to have really good pitch," she says. "Rod Temperton was able to have lots of chord changes while keeping the melody strong. The opening lyric, 'There'll be no darkness tonight, / lady our love will shine' is the only time that melody appears in the song. It never comes back.

Instead there are two other melody lines." The second and third verses have the same ethereal melody, while the bridge has a very different, funkier vibe, as does the tag where Michael improvises on that funky vamp.

Somewhere in the last third of the song, where Michael sings, "Stay with me / I want you to stay with me" and begins to riff, Santilli ends up singing and writhing on the floor. Laughing over the phone from Toronto, she suggests that the spirit of Michael must have moved through her. For Ivana, who grew up in Canada listening to the album, singing Michael Jackson live means you had to seriously commit, both in voice and on stage. For the evening, Ivana wears a *Thriller*-styled outfit—white suit, black shirt, leopard pocket square, and, in a nice extra retro touch, a haircut echoing Ola Ray in the famous "Thriller" video.

"Lady" is the last song on the album, but it is no throwaway. Originally commissioned by Quincy from Temperton as a possible song for Frank Sinatra, it has the tricky melodies and chord structure that first attracted Quincy to the Englishman's songwriting. Perhaps because of how it's written, "Lady" is not a song that radio programmers gravitated to in the wake of Michael's death. It may be more a singer's song than a fan's.

As challenging as Ivana found "Lady" to cover in 2009, Michael himself found it difficult to master for its original recording in 1983. In *Moon Walk* Michael wrote that it "was one of the most difficult tracks to cut. We were used to doing a lot of takes in order to get a vocal as nearly perfect as possible, but Quincy wasn't satisfied with my work on that song, even after literally dozens of takes. Finally he took me aside late one session and told me he wanted me to beg. That's what he said. He wanted me to go back in the studio and literally beg for it."

"It" in this case meant sex. For Michael, who'd grown up watching soul men beg on stage, it was a matter of tapping into that knowledge. Going back into the Westlake studio, Michael had the studio lights turned off and the curtains closed between the studio and the control room. "Q started the tape and I begged," he wrote. "The result is what you hear in the grooves." That prodding by Quincy resulted in a performance of technical precision and sensuality.

So "Lady in My Life" ends *Thriller* with a song that reflects Quincy's vision, Temperton's skill, and Michael's enormous vocal gifts. *Thriller,* the long-playing album, ends with Michael riding a laid-back rhythm. The record had ended, but the story was far from over.

PART 3

COVERING
THRILLER

N HIS ENTERTAINING MEMOIR OF RECORD BUSINESS
success and self-destruction, *Howling at the Moon*, ex–
Sony Music president Walter Yetnikoff wrote vividly of his
relationship with Michael Jackson and the sales of *Thriller.*
"No single record changed the business—and my life—as
powerfully as Michael Jackson's *Thriller*," Yetnikoff recalled.
"At one point the damn thing was selling a million copies a
week. I'd never seen such figures. Michael had once again
reinvented himself, only this time as the third prong of pop's
Holy Trilogy—now it was Elvis, the Beatles and Michael
Jackson."

During the height of *Thriller*, Yetnikoff said:

Michael's passion for world conquest was singular. . . . Michael's drive bordered on the psychopathic. He lived, breathed, slept, dreamt and spoke of nothing but number 1 successes. He was possessed. He'd call me night and day for the latest figures. . . . In the long period of its unprecedented success, however, when it occasionally fell to second place for a week or two, Michael panicked. Hysterical, he'd berate me for failing to up the promotion.

After reading Yetnikoff's memories of that time, I knew I needed to go back to the era myself.

In trying to recapture the journey of Michael Jackson's *Thriller* and his effect on the record industry during the period 1982–1985, I did something I hadn't in years: I read *Billboard* magazine. Not the current slick, graphic-heavy, twenty-first-century incarnation, but the *Billboard* of the 1980s that I had worked on, which was published on newsprint and aspired to break news. I remember the day computers were first brought into the *Billboard* newsroom to replace typewriters and my difficulty adjusting to the screen and the keyboard. That's how long ago in the world's technological cycle *Thriller* came out.

Looking through my Michael Jackson coverage at *Billboard,* and that of my colleagues in New York and Los Angeles, I could clearly see the direct impact and the subsequent ripple effect of *Thriller.* The pieces also brought back memories of what I had been doing and feeling while the *Thriller* wave rolled on. In addition, I looked through pieces I and others had written about *Thriller* during this remarkable time.

Initially, I traveled up to Manhattan's West Side to the Lincoln Center library, a place any New Yorker interested in researching American culture visits often, because of its vast collection of tapes, records, and microfilm. I peered at screens of *Billboard* starting in 1982. On the subway home, I remembered that years ago I'd filed away copies of my *Billboard* articles, but I had no idea where. Recently, I'd donated the research materials from several of my music books to the black music archive at Indiana University. I'd carried these boxes around with me through four apartments before finally sending all that work to a library in Bloomington, Indiana.

When I got home, I started digging through some of my remaining file cabinets, looking through magazines and pictures I hadn't touched in decades. There definitely was a part of me that wanted to file away my days as a dedicated vinyl junkie forever, and yet the presence of all those dented metal file cabinets brought me back to a part of my life I'd thought I'd outgrown. But here I was again, back in the world of the music critic, looking at an invitation to the listening party for Keith Sweat's *Make It Last Forever,* a promotional postcard for Public Enemy's *It Takes a Nation of Millions to Hold Us Back,* and a couple of Michael Jackson baseball cards.

At the bottom of a plastic packing crate filled with old Polaroids and datebooks was a wrinkled brown paper bag on which I'd scribbled "*Billboard* 1982 to 1989." Turns out I hadn't jettisoned all of my journalistic history. Moreover, as I began to read, I found that so many of the clippings stuffed into the brown paper bag documented the *Thriller* era.

As I read through them, several themes emerged: the impact on the business of *Thriller* as record and visual document; how some of the technical issues of the early 1980s in the record business echo today's downloading debate; Prince and hip-hop in relation to Jackson; the amount of controversy that surrounded the *Victory* tour; and larger economic issues. At the time, in the early years of the Reagan administration, the United States was in the middle of a recession that was hitting black folks especially hard. Upwardly mobile blacks with money tended, in postsegregation America, to shop in the same areas as whites of the same economic class. During the years of *Thriller*'s peak sales, this change had a lasting effect on the selling and making of black pop.

I'd joined *Billboard* in the spring of 1982, coming from *Record World,* a rival trade publication that had just gone out of business and where I'd been black music editor in 1981. My connection to *Billboard* went back to my college years. I'd interned there from 1977 to 1979, writing pieces for the disco section and talent reviews before, in 1979, being banned from the publication by the LA-based editor in chief for using "black English."

But by 1982 Adam White had taken over *Billboard*'s reins. Adam, a British soul music fanatic, had been one of my mentors on the staff when I was an intern and had watched me develop during my time at *Record World.* When I became available, Adam let go the writer heading the soul music coverage and brought me in as an editor and a writer of a weekly column I dubbed "The Rhythm and the Blues." It was from this comfortable perch that I watched *Thriller* change the game.

My column for May 22, 1982, titled "Jones Wrapping Summer; See Tie to Spielberg," was based on a long interview that I had done with Quincy for *Musician* magazine, a sister publication of *Billboard.* Most of the column focused on the Donna Summer album he was finishing.

Summer was one of the rare acts to emerge from disco who'd become a mainstream star, making the journey from the heavy-breathing vocals of "Love to Love You Baby" to mainstream pop such as "She Works Hard for the Money." As a black crossover star at the time, Summer was perceived as being on a par with Michael. Summer's core buyers were more likely to be white, and maybe gay, than black. So even though disco had become a dirty word by 1982, the legacy of that dance movement was everywhere, living a closeted life in plain sight. Quincy's Steven Spielberg connection would bear fruit in 1985 when, with Quincy serving as producer and composer, Spielberg directed his first full-on drama, an adaptation of Alice Walker's controversial black period novel *The Color Purple.*

IN THAT SAME MAY 22 ISSUE, I wrote a long piece, "Technology Impacts Black 'Sound': Producers Differ on Effect on Creativity, Spontaneity," that addressed the aesthetic changes technology was forcing on the sound of black pop. Whereas Stevie Wonder's experiments with the Moog synthesizer during the early 1970s had altered the balance between machine and live musicians, new toys where pushing the music toward another tipping point.

"The synthesizer is becoming more and more important in black music," said Kashif, who was then one of New York's hottest young producers, making hits for Evelyn King, Howard Johnson, and Melba Moore (he also produced his own work). "It's becoming a battle to see who can come up with the new sound or combination of sounds that will attract an audience. You're constantly experimenting with different rhythmic patterns, searching for something fresh." His model for the direction of black music was *Off the Wall*. He told me: "There has been such a concern on finding the right groove that you can hear where the melody and lyrics have been neglected. Look at Michael Jackson's *Off the Wall* LP. The entire package was a great merger of rhythm, lyric and melody. That's the reason it was so successful."

Cameo had once been a flashy, funky R&B band with as many as eleven members. But by 1984 the band was stripping down to a core trio, using the new emphasis on computer technology. "Now you have a wider range of colors," Larry Blackmon, Cameo's leader, producer, and frontman, told me. "We have all these new toys, yet you basically still record as you did years ago. The technology does make certain things easier to do. You still must have a vision. If you have no picture in mind, what difference does all the equipment make?" *Thriller* was created amid this revolution, and this classic album came down squarely on the analog side in terms of how it was engineered, though synthesizer, drum machines, and other tech toys were employed throughout.

In the June 5 issue, Cary Darling, a reporter based out of *Billboard*'s LA bureau, wrote a piece that really painted the landscape for music videos by black artists in the year before the MTV breakthrough by "Billie Jean." "Not long ago the terms 'black music' and 'video' seemed mutually exclusive," Darling wrote. "Rock acts were getting most of the video attention from record companies while the outlets for black music videos could be counted on one hand."

Of the new outlets for black videos mentioned in the piece, only one would have any staying power: "The Black Entertainment Television network is extending its programming service this summer with a major portion of time devoted to music," Darling wrote. In the twenty-first century, BET is the primary broadcast outlet for R&B/hip-hop acts, but in 1982 it was just about to assume that role.

Though most of the folks interviewed were optimistic about their ventures and about the expansion of the market for videos that MTV's presence represented, the anger so many in the world of black music felt about MTV's resistance to black artists bubbled up. "Can you seriously say that Stevie Wonder is just R&B?" asked Nancy Leiviska-Wild, video department head of Motown Records. "I'm offended by that. There are more outlets for black videos but I want to be where the hits are, not just the R&B videos."

The gift and the curse of black upward mobility and white corporate investment on black music were captured in a November 14 front article I wrote titled "Mom and Pop Stores Closing, but Music Holding Its Own." "While there are no hard figures available on the number of recently shuttered black-oriented retailers, conversations with surviving mom & pop operators suggest that those who fail are not being replaced," I reported. Bruce Webb, a feisty, outspoken record store owner in Philadelphia, observed: "It used to be that for every eight stores that went out of business, maybe five might come on in. People these days don't want to take that chance anymore."

Looking at the marketplace, I noted:

Albums by only three black acts have gone platinum [in 1982]; Quincy Jones' "The Dude," Diana Ross' "Why Do Fools Fall in Love?" and Al Jarreau's "Breakin' Away." That makes up only 7% of this year's total to date, compared to 18% in all of 1981. However the relative stability of black sales is suggested by the fact that 18% of the 92 albums certified gold this year were by black acts, with two months to go. The proportion was 22% for all of 1981 and 23% in 1980.

An important factor in both the demise of many small black-oriented retailers and the consistent sales of black acts is the greater involvement of general market retail chains in selling this type of music.

As Hank Caldwell, a marketing vice president for the Warner Bros. Records group, said: "I've found awareness among chain stores that black music is growing. They are more willing to get involved in promotions with black acts and to do in stores."

This evolution in the willingness of white retail chains to support black artists would be reflected in the sales of *Thriller* in 1983 and subsequently in the massive album sales of Whitney Houston, Lionel Richie, and Prince, all of whom would make their own multiplatinum breakthroughs during a golden age of black pop acts selling vinyl and cassettes across the board. In the early 1970s, soul music had shifted from a singles-oriented business to an album-driven business. The difference between the two decades, however, was that the audience for these 1970s acts purchased through predominantly black-owned retailers, whereas Michael and others presaged a new order where the Tower Records of the world showcased black stars and middle-class black consumers shopped.

In my November 14 article, Richard Allen, a vice president for R&B promotion at Arista Records, commented that the growth of independent black music labels "has helped and will continue to aid small retailers and the sale of black music, since they have more time for person-to-person contact with them and, as small businesses themselves, can understand their problems better than a conglomerate." This opening in the marketplace for the mom and pop stores that survived this era would be filled primarily by two types of music: gospel and hip-hop (in the northeast Caribbean, reggae-socca would be a factor). These two styles of African American expression—one of religious fervor, one of materialist desire—would be life preservers for scores of black-owned businesses. These stores, which were of scant interest to the major labels, would support hip-hop until, a decade later, it, too, fulfilled its crossover dreams.

ANOTHER MENTION OF *THRILLER* came in *Billboard*'s October 2 issue in a column titled "Quincy Jones Get Extra-Terrestrial." The main focus here was a children's recording of an adaptation of Spielberg's science fiction megahit *E.T.: The Extra-Terrestrial*, with Quincy producing and Michael Jackson narrating. "Sources close to the trio say this album is a prelude to a cinematic collaboration between Jones, Jackson and Spielberg in the near future," I wrote. At the time the big rumor was that Michael would play Peter Pan in a film adaptation of that children's classic. (Spielberg would eventually do a Peter Pan film called *Hook* in 1991, but without either of his *E.T.* musical partners.)

Thriller was mentioned in the story's last paragraph: "Meanwhile, back on earth, Jackson's new Jones produced album *Thriller* is due out in mid-November. The album isn't finished yet, despite reports to the contrary, and even the Jackson-Paul McCartney single 'The Girl is Mine' is still having strings and other sweetening added."

154

My December 18 column, "Prince Agrees to Talk—a Little," focused on a *Los Angeles Times* interview with the usually closed mouth singer-songwriter. While dispelling some rumors (yes, his name was Prince Rogers Nelson; no, he wasn't gay), the Minneapolis native couldn't help but perpetuate his mystique: "I'm not Jamie Starr," he said, which was the supposed name of a Twin Cities producer who worked with Prince and his acolytes. But, in fact, Prince was Jamie Starr. It was one of several playful pseudonyms (such as Alexander Nevermind) that Prince employed to toy with nosy reporters and titillate his fans.

Prince's bold closing quote threw a gauntlet down before his competition. "The most important thing is to be true to yourself, but I also like the danger. That's what's missing from pop music today. There's no excitement and mystery; people sneaking out and going to see Elvis Presley or Jimi Hendrix," he told Robert Hilburn. "I'm not saying I'm better than anyone else but I don't feel like there are a lot of people out there telling the truth in their music."

At the very end of my column, almost as an afterthought, was a minireview of *Thriller.* (I must have gotten an advance cassette just before I had to file my column.) That I squeezed a review in instead of waiting a week meant I was anxious to get in my two cents early. And knowing about the brewing Prince–Michael Jackson rivalry, I'm sure I thought it delicious to put the review at the end of a Prince column, where I was certain both men would notice it.

I wrote then: "Michael Jackson's *Thriller* may not be as

strong as *Off the Wall*, but it is still one of 1982's best albums with several exceptional cuts. 'Human Nature,' 'Beat It,' and 'Billie Jean' are real standouts. The latter is, at least to these ears, an instant classic with its potent melody, arrangement and lyric." That I didn't think *Thriller* was as good as *Off the Wall* reflects conventional music connoisseur wisdom these days, but it was very much my initial impression.

THROUGHOUT THE SPRING OF 1983, my *Billboard* colleagues and I covered the early sales success of *Thriller,* but it was far from the only thing going on in the record business. Following up *Off the Wall* and the Paul McCartney duet, the album was expected to perform. Then on May 16, 1983, the *Motown 25* special aired on NBC and Michael moonwalked into pop cultural history. A few weeks after that appearance, I received a phone call from an editor at Dell Publishing. Did I want to write a book about Michael Jackson? Apparently Geri Hirshey, the *Rolling Stone* reporter who'd done a well-observed cover story on Michael that spring, had turned down the deal. Quickie rock bios were in vogue at the time, after Dave Marsh's *Born to Run*, about Bruce Springsteen, and Jerry Hopkins and Danny Sugerman's book on Jim Morrison, *No One Here Gets Out Alive*, had both made the *New York Times* best-seller list.

I was the second choice (I believe) for the book, and I signed on quickly. My dream at the time was to write a book about Motown Records, so this seemed a great practice for the real deal. Moreover, Dell was paying $7,000 in 1984 dollars, which I hoped would help me get my first solo apartment. Throughout the summer of 1983, as I was performing my regular *Billboard* duties, I was interviewing people about Michael Jackson. It was a strange journey. There were lots of people who wanted to talk about Michael—success has many fathers—but the most interesting stuff was always off the record.

Several people remarked on the young man's dichotomy. On one hand, the singer was an amazing case of arrested development. His demeanor, his childlike love of cartoons, what made him laugh, and what he talked about suggested that he was fourteen, not coming up on twenty-five. On the other hand, he had an intense, very adult quality that manifested itself in his work ethic, career strategies, and understanding of songwriting. I'd hear stories of Michael wandering around Encino on foot at night (unusual in California) for reasons unknown, and then people would speak in awe of his focus in the studio. It sometimes felt as if he were two men. The closest comparison is the depiction of Wolfgang Amadeus Mozart in the film *Amadeus* (released in September 1984), in which the classical composer is both a coarse child and a musical genius.

However, almost none of that complexity made it into the completed book. The manuscript I turned in that fall was probably twice as long as the final book. The editor excised anything too thoughtful, vaguely controversial, or musically observant. But I couldn't complain that much. It was my first book, and I needed the money.

IT WAS NOVEMBER 1983, after I'd delivered my manuscript to Dell and was going through final copyedits, when a press conference was held in Central Park's Tavern on the Green to announce details of a tour that would feature Michael and his brothers. Tavern on the Green was a big, garish tourist trap of a restaurant located on Central Park West and West 67th Street. Its main feature was a high–windowed, atrium-styled dining area, which was filled with media from around the globe. Various Jackson family members were in attendance, including Katherine, Joe, and Jermaine's gorgeous wife, Margaret Maldonado.

Michael and his brothers emerged from behind curtains and sitting on a riser and then took seats at a long conference table. They all wore aviator-styled shades and various multi-colored outfits that suggested their style hadn't changed much since their days in the Jackson 5. Though obviously the main attraction, Michael sat at the far right of the dais. It was the first time I recall seeing him in one of the drum major/military dictator uniforms that would eventually replace the red jacket as his trademark look. That outfit was actually Michael's most dramatic statement of the press conference; otherwise, he said little and often looked either uncomfortable or uninterested, perhaps both.

Chuck Sullivan, a Boston-based businessman whose family owned the National Football League's New England Patriots, had originally been the promoter of what was likely the most anticipated concert tour of the decade. But Sullivan was inexperienced in the world of music and concert promotion, leaving an opening for others to seize.

The "other" in this case was loquacious, nefarious boxing promoter Don King. By appealing to Joe and Katherine with pleas of black pride and his expertise in running massive events, King emerged as the tour's spokesperson and chief promoter. It was King, with his two-paragraph sentences and grandiose persona, who dominated the press conference, giving credence to the idea that he was using this *Victory* tour to move into the realm of concert promotion. Pepsi, which was already getting into business with Michael via commercials, would come on board as a sponsor.

But, overall, details were sketchy and would remain so through the spring of 1984. Among King, Sullivan, local promoters, and various other players (record mogul/talent manager Irving Azoff would grab control of the lucrative merchandising rights), the run-up to the tour would be a mess of rumors, backstage infighting, and bad vibes. After all the careful thought and preparation that had gone into the making of *Thriller,* the *Victory* tour would have a half-assed quality about it.

The high ticket prices, with many seats more than $100, which was unprecedented at the time, rankled the parents of many of Michael's fans and created a backlash against the tour organizers' perceived greed. By bowing to pressure from his parents and brothers, Michael would embark on a tour that earned millions and, unfortunately, put an enduring taint on his name. After the Tavern on the Green press conference, Michael slipped out of a side entrance and left in a limo alone.

THE FIRE,
THE TOUR

M ICHAEL AND *THRILLER* WERE ALREADY MAKING
history at the start of the year novelist George Orwell predicted would find the world controlled by
thought police and an omnipresent figure called Big Brother,
the leader of an oppressive government known as "the Party."
In Orwell's *1984*, Big Brother's image is projected on huge
screens, a figure no one can escape. Michael's image wasn't
quite that ubiquitous in the real 1984, but his visibility ri-
valed even that of President Ronald Reagan. In these fateful
twelve months, Michael's life, musical and otherwise, dominated the cultural conversation.

My slender quickie biography, *The Michael Jackson Story*,
reached bookstores within days of January 27, when

Michael's hair caught on fire while he was taping a Pepsi commercial at LA's Shrine Auditorium. Before the footage leaked on YouTube right after his death, it was very closely guarded. But anyone can now see the biggest pop star on the planet dance for several anxious seconds before realizing his jheri curl was ablaze.

It was a horrific moment, made even worse because this accident was a turning point in Michael's life. In every account of Michael's life after this accident, friends and business associates confirm that this is when Michael first started taking painkillers, which would lead to a long-term addiction to prescription drugs that would incapacitate and, ultimately, kill him.

Apart from this long-term consequence of the Pepsi fire, a more immediate short-term issue was Michael's skin and hair. Since Michael was a child, various family members had made fun of his large nose, perhaps to keep the young star's ego in check and maintain the pecking order of the family. Whatever the motivation, this teasing still nagged at him as a young adult. He also complained about his acne and the self-consciousness that produced.

Sometime between *Off the Wall* and *Thriller,* Michael had a nose job. A simple comparison of the two album covers confirms that he did. His skin tone also seemed redder than just a few years before. But after the Pepsi fire, the changes to his skin tone and facial structure intensified. Once he altered his face and lost contact with his original features, there was no turning back.

There's a strong argument to be made that without these cosmetic changes, Michael would not have been the global star he became, that the consistent lightening of his face throughout the 1980s was a huge part of what made him most palatable to non-Americans. Although Americans, white as well as black, were obsessed with the radical changes in his appearance, the international audiences that passionately supported him, and continue to do so to this day, were never as concerned about how he used to look. They accepted Michael's white face in a way that Americans never have. Many African Americans saw his changing color as a sign of betrayal, of self-hate. White American detractors viewed him as a freak (e.g., "Wacko Jacko") whose skin lightening was another example of his weirdness. The rest of the world was both less judgmental and more open-minded. In the summer after his death, I traveled around Europe, visiting cities in Spain and Italy, and saw many visual memorials to Michael, all of them featuring him as he appeared with lighter skin. In tributes to Michael in China, India, eastern Europe, and South America, that same vision of Michael abounded. Unaffected by America's tortured racial history, global ticket buyers would come to view the post-*Thriller* Michael as the one who truly mattered.

GLOBAL DOMINATION WAS the focus of an event I attended, along with 1,500 others, in New York City just eleven days after the accident in Los Angeles. On February 7 at the

Museum of Natural History, CBS Records organized an extravagant party to celebrate Michael's inclusion in the Guinness Book of World Records for the still-soaring sales of *Thriller*. Despite the accident just a few days before, Michael looked good, with perhaps a bit too much rouge on his cheeks.

For me, going to an event at which Brooke Shields walked alongside Michael, holding his gloved hand, was quite exciting. Like so many of the public events Michael would attend during this period, he said little (certainly nothing very revealing or surprising), but just the fact he was in the building gave the event an air of importance.

My association with *Thriller* changed my life. The book was excerpted in major newspapers around the country. I was fielding tons of interview requests about Michael's career. At the same time, many West Coast, Motown, or Michael-associated record business folks seemed to put me on their enemies list, even though the book was benign and quite celebratory in tone.

Right after my quickie bio, the publishing floodgates opened and Michael Jackson books of every description were not just published, but also joined mine on the *New York Times* best-seller list. The appetite for information about Michael was insatiable and global. My book ended up being published in the United Kingdom, Japan, and Spain. Unable to reach Michael through official channels, many fans sent me letters that they either wanted me to pass on to Michael or that they addressed to the artist himself. It was a dizzying time for me and is still a blur twenty-five years later.

On February 28, on the same stage where he'd been burned almost a month before, Michael dominated the Grammys, winning eight awards, including producer of the year (shared with Quincy), record of the year for "Billie Jean," and album of the year for *Thriller.* He and Quincy even won one for the *ET* children's album. This night was the peak of Michael's career and, perhaps, of his life. The sales were incredible, and with that came artistic credibility and the respect of his peers.

It's worth taking a step back to look at the pop culture landscape Michael now ruled. Today we accept as given that black performers can easily become global pop figures. But Michael was the harbinger. On January 4, 1984, Oprah Winfrey made her debut as co-host of *AM Chicago,* her first appearance in a city she would come to define. In February, Whoopi Goldberg made her New York City stage debut in *The Spook Show.* The same month Run-D.M.C.'s self-titled debut hit record stores, and in June the "Fresh Fest" tour, the first national showcase for New York rappers and breakers, went on a twenty-seven-city tour. On June 19, the Chicago Bulls made Michael Jordan its number one choice in the NBA draft. On September 20, *The Cosby Show* debuted on NBC. On December 5, Eddie Murphy, already a star, became a superstar when *Beverly Hills Cop* opened around the nation.

A wave of African American talent, coming from very different places and points of view, had massive mainstream appeal by 1984. All of these artists became so accepted collectively that they would reshape the African American image and render no dream too big. Did Michael, Oprah, and Eddie eventually set the stage for the first black president? That's a big leap to make (George Bush's inadequacies had an awful lot to do with the 2008 election). But did this exciting landscape inspire a young Barack Obama to say, "Yes, I can"?

The Shrine Auditorium, which was partially designed by black Los Angeles architect Paul Williams, located just across the street from the University of Southern California in traditionally black South Central, was where the past and future of Michael Jackson came together in January and February 1984. The Pepsi fire made him even more famous and would, in a tragic way, alter his life, whereas the Grammy Awards was the summation of his training, hard work, and vision.

From the mountaintop, there is no place else to go but down. Michael was twenty-five the night of the Grammys. It had taken him twenty or so years of performing to reach that moment. It was rare air he breathed, but it would never be quite that sweet again.

IN AN ACKNOWLEDGMENT of Michael's star power, Ronald and Nancy Reagan feted Michael in the Rose Garden on May 17, 1984, to thank him for donating the use of "Beat It" in an anti–drunk driving public service announcement. But it was really just an elaborate photo opportunity featuring one great entertainer sucking up to another. Michael wore a glittery military outfit with shades and glove on his right hand as the first lady grinned for the cameras.

Considering Reagan's antipoor policies and cutbacks in social programs, as well as the plague of crack already permeating black neighborhoods nationwide, Michael didn't have or need to make this appearance. He'd never shown any serious interest in politics before, and it would have been a real shock if he'd started in the Rose Garden. Nevertheless, in the year that Reverend Jesse Jackson (a man who'd given the Jackson 5 an early showcase at an Operation Push fund-raiser in Chicago) was mounting his electrifying first campaign for president, Michael didn't have to give the GOP's leader the tacit approval the visit suggested. But for Michael the White House seal of approval was more important than any other consideration.

IN THE MONTHS LEADING UP to the *Victory* tour, conflicting reports about when it would start and where it would go and complaints about ticket distribution filled the media. A national mail order system was used for a time, making it difficult for someone to just walk up to a ticket window and purchase a ticket. In fact, initially you were required to buy four tickets if you were using mail order.

"My girls were among the millions who grew up loving the Jackson Five," Vertamae Grosvenor spoke for many in a National Public Radio commentary. "They tore pictures out of *Jet* and *Right On!* magazine. [But] I will not go to a concert: can't afford it—thirty dollars a ticket." Grosvenor, a black woman writer and author, added: "I am disturbed by the cosmetic change. . . . Now, like a growing number of black performers, Michael has had his nose fixed. He's exotic, non-threatening. Seems to be the way to go to crossover. It's the kind of sexuality America likes in her black stars, especially the men."

That spring I had a rather strange interview with Jermaine Jackson. Jermaine had left Motown for Arista Records, had reunited with his brothers, and was beginning to emerge as the most prominent spokesperson for all the Jacksons. We had a mutual friend in John McClain, the Jacksons' childhood friend, but the publication of my book had put a strain on that relationship. Because of the book, I wasn't sure if Jermaine would sit with me, but, after all, he did have a record of his own to promote.

We met out at a studio in the Valley. Jermaine was cordial but a little tense, and he made a big deal of bringing out his own tape recorder to show that he was recording our conversation, too. Most of the article I subsequently wrote about the interview focused on his new album, an as-yet-untitled Arista debut. Reading it now, I see that a duet with "recent Arista signee Whitney Houston" merited only a passing mention.

The last third of the article focused on the *Victory* tour and the controversy about Don King:

> There is no one else in the business right now who could take this tour out other than Don King. No one. He may bring on other promoters to help him, but they'll be no other promoters, because he has the contracts on us. That's the bottom line.
>
> The reason we went with Don King was that he was talking about bringing the family together. He included my mother and father as part of this team, and now he's in partnership with them. That's what we loved about him.

I asked Jermaine about a recent *Rolling Stone* piece attacking King and the Jacksons' organization of the tour. He replied, "I don't think anything in that article spoke the truth about my family."

One morning not long after that interview with Jermaine, I received a phone call at home from Katherine and Joe Jackson. I was shocked. It was about 9 a.m. New York time, so the call came very early from the West Coast. The call wasn't about the book, but about the tour. They wanted me to make a statement on their behalf regarding what was going on with the tour, and because I was the black reporter at *Billboard,* they came to me. What I remember most was the tone of the talk.

Both Joe and Katherine felt very embattled and resentful of the sort of coverage they'd received. They presented themselves as simply concerned parents trying to look out for their children, nothing more or less, though they were not innocents in the situation. They'd been pursuing the show business dream for some twenty years at that time. They had to know that bringing in Don King to work on the tour, no matter what he promised them, would introduce an element of controversy, something that followed the flamboyant promoter wherever he went.

The July 21 issue of *Billboard,* published the week the *Victory* tour kicked off in Kansas City, contained an insert tribute to Michael titled "The Saga of Michael Jackson" and written by *Los Angeles Times* pop music critic Robert Hilburn. The cover was a full-color picture of Michael, and the inside of the cover contained a gatefold Pepsi ad. The tribute insert was forty pages long and was filled with full-page ads from old friends (Diana Ross, Lionel Richie, Smokey Robinson) and current business partners (Paul and Linda McCartney, CBS, Vestron Home Video, Don King).

Paul Grein, *Billboard*'s talent editor, wrote the front-page story on the business aspect of the tour, headlined "Jacksons' Tour Starts Smoothly," with the subhead "No Violence in Kansas City." Grein reported:

Widespread concern that the concerts might be marred by violence proved unfounded, though security was nearly as tight as it might be for the visit of a President or a Pope. Tour promoter Chuck Sullivan says he spent five times as much money for security as he would for an average football game. And the backlash that seemed to be developing against the tour in the weeks leading up to the first date appeared to have stopped with the July 5 announcement that the national mail order system for obtaining tickets was being scrapped.

Much of the piece went into great detail about the hows and whys of ticket sales and indicated that local promoters, including several African Americans, were being added in cities such as New York and Dallas. Interestingly, Grein didn't mention Don King; Chuck Sullivan was apparently the point man with the trade media. In a sidebar, Grein complained about the show's 105-minute running time, which crystallized the beef of many: "Once the Jacksons lengthen the show, at least past the two hour mark, they should consider splitting it into two sets. If they're not willing to do that, they should at least add a name act (the Pointer Sisters for example) to open the show. If you're asking the audience to spend $30 for a ticket, you should at least give them a full evening's entertainment, complete with an intermission."

Perhaps the most memorable thing about that July 21 issue had everything and nothing to do with Michael Jackson. The issue's back cover featured purple raindrops falling against a royal blue ski. The ad inside read: "Warner Bros. Records Takes Great Pride in the Success of 'Purple Rain.' Platinum Upon Release, the Album contains 'When Doves Cry,' the fastest selling single in the History of Warner Bros.

Records. The Film 'Purple Rain' Premieres this month at Select Theaters Nationwide. The Rain Has Just Begun."

The magazine then opened up to display a poster-sized ad for *Purple Rain,* the album and movie, featuring an iconic shot of Prince sitting on a motorcycle at the backstage door of the First Avenue nightclub in Minneapolis, with Apollonia looking sultry in the doorway. As a bit of strategic one–upmanship, the ad was a beautiful thing and let the industry know that Warner Bros. was going to pull out all the stops to make the album an event.

I SAW THE *VICTORY* TOUR three times in 1984, each a very different experience. The tour opened at Kansas City's Arrowhead Stadium on July 6. The atmosphere around the tour's official hotel, where I picked up my tickets, felt like a carnival, with vendors of Michael memorabilia, obsessed fans in red jackets and glittering gloves, and lots of folks scalping tickets to willing buyers. Rumors where rife: Michael was too sick to perform; Michael hated his brothers so much he wouldn't go onstage; counterfeit tickets had flooded the market.

In a large ballroom, a brief, weird press conference was held with Don King, again, rambling on about the magnificence of the show. Michael came on stage, waved his hand to the crowd, and then disappeared. The Arrowhead Stadium parking lot, an extension of the area around the hotel, was filled with hard-core Jackson fanatics mixed in with families there just because the kids wanted to come.

I wrote about my experience at the concert in the *Village Voice:*

As [the Kansas City] concert testified, Michael is the first black star of his generation to follow Bill Cosby and Mr. T into the kindergartens and bridge tournaments of our vast country. For those Americans, *Victory* is like going to the Ice Capades. No dangerous adolescent list or unbridled urban anger rippled through the crowd that beautiful still evening in the heartland. Instead we had kids spending much of the time looking at a huge TV screen to ascertain whether the doll-like stick figure wiggling in the distance was indeed Michael. Parents like the ones sitting behind me getting loudly drunk and spilling beer on my shoes enjoyed the spectacle of it, though the only non-"Thriller" material they seemed to know came during the Jackson Five medley. They were looking for family entertainment; a little sentiment, a little fantasy, a little dancing, a little nostalgia, a lot of glitter.

As the first show of a large tour, the Kansas City, Missouri, date felt like "a glorified rehearsal," with the tempos on several songs ("Off the Wall" and "Human Nature," for example) too fast. Most disappointing was that the staging of the songs from the Jacksons' albums and *Off the Wall* was pretty much performed as it had been on the *Triumph* tour. The Jacksons performed none of the new material from the *Victory* album, though the avowed purpose of the tour was to showcase the talents of the "other" brothers. At none of the three shows I attended was Marlon, Tito, or the gifted Randy showcased. (Jackie, injured and on crutches, had a good excuse.) The truth, of course, was that this was a Michael Jackson solo tour, nothing more or less.

After the show, I rushed back to my hotel to catch *Nightline*, because I'd been interviewed for a package in the tour. I don't remember what I said or much else about that half-hour show, other than I felt part of some huge national event unlike anything in pop music before.

The second concert I attended was at Giants Stadium in the New Jersey Meadowlands, and it was a remarkable show. The crowd, which was much more integrated than the KC gig had been, was treated to a supertight rhythm section, a better laser show, and some fresh bits of choreography. But the real difference was Michael, who seemed more engaged than at that opening show. "Michael was as aggressive, fiery and macho as any '60s soul man," I wrote in the *Village Voice*.

With a sneering intense scowl on his face, Michael shook his pelvis, moonwalked and sang with heart and a whole lot of deep-fried soul. The contrast with Kansas City was stark. There he seemed a fairy prince off in the distance, far removed and detached from his subjects and even the show itself. In Jersey he walked the waterfront with a chip on his shoulder, moving and singing with real blood in his eye.

This was particularly true of the show's first half, when even during "She's Out of My Life" he threw in some break dance movements, signifying that on this night all sweetness must be cut with funk. It might have been that Jersey swampland air, but more likely it was that Michael, like his band, was now in mid-tour form and fully ready to justify to the skeptical just how much he was worth. I wondered, looking at the family of four in front of me, whether Mom and Pop were quite ready for this Michael, a cat who would just as soon have kicked the ass of those gang leaders in "Beat It" as started a chorus line. Springsteen may be the boss and Prince the royal contender, but guess who still wears the crown.

The last show of the tour I saw was at Madison Square Garden in late August, and, quite honestly, it felt tired. Unlike the 1981 show at that same venue, which had been bursting with energy, this performance felt like a group of men punching a clock. Michael, in particular, seemed tired and remote. This was my third, and final, time seeing Michael with his brothers at Madison Square Garden, and it left no memory other than one of exhaustion. I'd spent too much of the year as a resident Michael Jackson expert and had written about him for the *Village Voice* and *Musician* as well as doing my regular duties at *Billboard.* Though some embraced this role, I had no interest in writing solely about Michael Jackson for the rest of my career.

Besides, as 1984 unfolded, Prince and hip-hop and *The Cosby Show* were shifting the focus of media folks like myself. There was so much going on, so many doors opening. I had finally started in earnest to work on the Motown book I had long dreamed of. I knew it was time to get off the Michael Jackson bandwagon and find out who I was as a writer.

THE *BAD* YEARS

I N THE SUMMER OF 1987, STREET CULTURE, IN ITS most brutal and creative forms, was beginning its long reign as the cutting edge of pop culture. Crack, the fast food of addictive drugs, was transforming parents into dope fiends and urban street corners into combat zones. Forty-six percent of black children were living below the poverty line in 1987, the highest number since the mid-1960s. They were living in the chaos, and they were writing about it.

This year hip-hop, which had been making inroads into the national consciousness for several years, yielded several of its greatest street poets: KRS-One, Ice T, Big Daddy Kane, Chuck D, and Rakim brought new levels of complexity, politics, and narrative to the burgeoning genre. The leadership in black music was shifting from LA glitz to New York grit, and Michael, though already planning to buy the isolated Neverland Ranch in Santa Barbara, California, was very aware that he'd have to address this change in his follow-up to *Thriller.*

Strangely, Michael's desire to stay current and my journalistic career would end up intersecting again. Two years before the release of *Bad,* I covered a tragic story for the *Village Voice.* Edmund Perry, a bright, charismatic boy from West 114th Street, a hard, blighted block in crack-infested Harlem, was fatally wounded by police officer Lee Van Houten in Morningside Park on the night of June 12, 1985. Perry had been attending Phillips Exeter Academy in New Hampshire as part of ABC (A Better Chance), a program that since 1964 had been sending inner-city boys and girls to prep schools on full scholarship. He and his brother, Jonah, who was attending Westminster School in Connecticut, had been given golden tickets out of the 'hood. But on this hot summer night, Van Houten, a cop just two years on the force, accused the teenagers of having tried to mug him in the park and claimed he'd shot Edmund in self-defense.

Stepping out of the music world, I investigated the shooting by talking to cops, family members, and classmates and by walking through the park where Edmund had died. Many people, including colleagues at the *Voice,* took as a given that the Perry brothers had attempted to mug the plainclothes cop. But my reporting suggested there was much more than a reasonable doubt involved in this use of deadly force and that NYPD had lied about several key details of the shooting and the aftermath. In "Why Did Edmund Perry Die?" I wrote:

Central to the official version is not just Van Houten's testimony but the assumption that Edmund's background meant nothing—that when Edmund saw the chance to mug a white person he took it. Really, what other motivation would a young nigger need? Motivation is precisely what's missing from the police account, and they seem to be aware of this. . . . Since Edmund's death eight young people, all residents of 114th Street, have been picked up by the police and questioned not about the shooting, but about Edmund's character.

In the view of Edmund Perry's family, he was in the wrong place at the wrong time and he was the victim of either a mistake or a cold-blooded murder and cover up. The questions they and (attorney) Vernon Mason have raised don't establish Edmund's innocence, but they cast doubt on the police account.

After the article ran, the *New York Times* weighed in with a story heavily slanted to make Edmund look like a budding young drug dealer up at a white prep school. Yet Jonah was not indicted for assault. Moreover, I learned much later that the city had reached an out-of-court settlement with the family. Jonah went on to attend Cornell, where an older sister was a student. While the family made peace with this horrible shooting, the story of a black Harlemite at a New England prep school who died under violent circumstances took on a life of its own, generating a book and a made-for-TV movie and helping to inspire the video for "Bad."

MARTIN SCORSESE, a master filmmaker and New York homeboy, got celebrated crime writer Richard Price to build the frame of the story from Edmund's life. The black-and-white establishing story has Michael as a teenager at a prep school on the last day of school. A white classmate tells Michael he's proud of him; coming at the end of the semester, this remark is a sign of Michael's slow acceptance by his peers. In a great bit of visual storytelling, Scorsese contrasts a ride on the New Haven train line filled with boisterous white high schoolers with Michael headed to the second part of his journey, a ride uptown in a crowded subway car populated by expressionless people.

Back on his Harlem block, Michael runs into three homies in front of his apartment building. One of the trio, the gang's chief instigator, is played by Wesley Snipes, a fine young actor just four years away from becoming a major movie star in *New Jack City* and *Jungle Fever*. After a wordless confrontation with a local drug dealer, Wesley goads Michael into joining his mugging crew. Just as the four boys are about to rob an old man, Michael changes his mind. In the ensuing confrontation, the footage shifts from black and white to color and the dance part of the *Bad* video begins.

Under the guidance of Scorsese, and definitely pushed by Snipes's acting chops, Michael gives a very credible performance as the Edmund Perry–like character. Michael's naturally soft voice and otherworldly persona make for a convincing fish out of water, both at prep school and in a Harlem stairwell. Though by 1987 he was considerably paler than during the *Thriller* era, there's still a lot of expressiveness in his face. Prodded by Snipes, who'd go on to create the iconic gangsta Nino Brown and who possessed a dark, expressive face and insinuating delivery, Michael suggested that he could have had a career in motion pictures if he'd been able to work with directors of Scorsese's caliber (not that there are many like the director of *Raging Bull*).

The dance sequence, which was shot just one subway stop away from my home station in Brooklyn, is fun but does convey a mixed message. On one hand, the framing story is a pretty raw dose of hard-bitten New York noir. Even the way the supporting dancers are dressed reflects the impact of hip-hop on clothing. On the other hand, Michael's black ensemble, lined with zippers and buckles, is more Melrose Avenue than downtown Brooklyn.

Apparently, "Bad" was originally intended as a duet between Michael and Prince, but the Minneapolis star ignored the offer. The song seems more like a speeded-up, R&B cover of LL Cool J's "I'm Bad" than an original track. But the video's coda, where Michael does a lengthy call-and-response improv with the dancers, playing on the "bad" title as a challenge to Snipes's character, is beautifully soulful and is as close to a gospel sermon as Michael ever delivered on camera.

THE SUPPORTING *BAD* TOUR, Michael's first solo tour, was far superior to the *Victory* tour on several levels. The band, composed solely of top "road dawgs" (professional touring musicians), was much tighter and more versatile, and they played a lot of the fine songs on *Bad.* Of the three Quincy Jones–produced solo albums, *Bad* is usually overshadowed by *Off the Wall* and *Thriller.* Yet song for song, it is probably the deepest of the Jackson/Jones trilogy.

Brimming with confidence in his ability, Michael's songwriting dominates the album. No Rod Temperton songs made the album. Nor is there any song as genre busting as "Beat It" or as intense as "Billie Jean." What is on *Bad* are songs with magnificent melodies ("I Just Can't Stop Loving You," "Liberian Girl"), cinematic in conception ("Smooth Criminal"), and smartly funky ("The Way You Make Me Feel," "Another Part of Me"). The secret hero of *Bad* is singer-songwriter Siedah Garrett, who sang the female part on "I Just Can't Stop Loving You" and co-wrote the song that would become an anthem for Michael, both before and after his death.

Garrett is a tremendously talented artist who has never quite become a star, yet has had a remarkable career nonetheless. In 1984 she sang a duet with ex-Temptations lead singer Dennis Edwards on a song titled "Don't Look Any Further." Edwards, who sang on a number of classic Temptations hits after replacing David Ruffin as lead singer of that vocal group, had floundered as a solo act. But this song became a massive R&B hit and a staple to this day on any classic soul format on broadcast or the Internet.

The song went down as a hit for Dennis Edwards, while Siedah grew a reputation as a background singer and songwriter. Like so many talented performers in Los Angeles during that period, Siedah came to the attention of Quincy Jones. At the time of the recording of *Bad,* Quincy was preparing her solo album for his Qwest label. On her way to the studio to record her vocals for "I Just Can't Stop Loving You" she paused at a traffic light and glanced at herself in the mirror. She could have titled the song "Woman in the Mirror," but knowing she was heading to a session for Michael Jackson, Siedah thought the male pronoun made more sense.

Collaborating with Los Angeles producer-writer Glen Ballard (who'd become famous in a few years for producing Alanis Morissette's *Jagged Little Pill*), Siedah wrote a lyric that is part self-help philosophy, part plea for brotherhood, and full of instantly memorable imagery. Supported by a powerhouse choir arrangement by gospel great Andraé Crouch, "Man in the Mirror" soars and inspires like many pop songs aspire to but few achieve. In the days after Michael's death, "Man in the Mirror" was his second most downloaded song (after "Thriller"). More than 165,000 people bought it between June 25 and 28, more than "Billie Jean" and all the other big hits. It was the song played as his body was taken out of the Staples Center at the end of his memorial service. Though Michael didn't write "Man in the Mirror," the song is as connected to his life as any he ever recorded.

In March 1988 at Madison Square Garden, "Man in the Mirror" was the eighteenth and final song of the show I attended. I was with my eight-year-old niece, Eboni, who, like every child I've ever known, was a huge Michael Jackson fan. Unlike the arrangement in the *Victory* tour, Michael's videos were folded seamlessly into the show, so that costume changes and lighting cues incorporated the red jacket, the glittering glove and socks, the tuxedo, and the treasure trove of iconography from ten years of his videos. To this day, only Madonna can challenge Michael Jackson as a creator of a visual vocabulary as rich in association.

One of my most vivid memories of the *Bad* concert at Madison Square Garden was making sure my niece wasn't freaked out by *Thriller.* Back in 1984, Eboni was one of the thousands of kids for whom Michael's transformation into a werewolf and a zombie was overwhelming. "Michael Jackson is not a monster!" she cried when I first showed her my early copy of the video.

"Michael Jackson is not a monster!" echoed in my head for years afterward. The Michael Jackson who had dueted on "I Just Can't Stop Loving You" with then-unknown background singer Sheryl Crow at the Garden some twenty-one years ago seemed lighter on this night than he had even in the *Bad* video.

In his early videos, Michael's touch, his very presence, could transform reality and bring order to chaos. Now his body itself would be transformed. Though after his death the African American community closed ranks around his memory, back in the late 1980s Michael's skin tone changes made him a lightning rod for criticism from pulpits to barbershops. Michael would claim later these changes came as he tried to compensate for an extreme case of the skin disease vitiligo. But the re-creation of his face, which encompassed a radical reshaping of his nose, was beyond what the disease could have caused.

In a surprisingly frank interview right after Michael's death, Quincy talked with *Details* magazine's Jeff Gordinier about the singer's evolution. "Oh, we talked about it all the time," Quincy said. "But he'd come up with 'Man, I promise you I have this disease' and so forth, and 'I have a blister on my lungs,' and all that kind of b.s. It's hard, because Michael's a Virgo, man—he's very set in his ways. You can't talk him out of it. Chemical peels and all that stuff." Quincy even suggested, in a very sad way, that Michael had issues about his blackness.

"Leave Me Alone," the last song on the *Bad* album, is Michael's side of the story. Using a hook ("Stop doggin' me around") that paid homage to one of Jackie Wilson's signature hits, "Leave Me Alone" had the paranoia of "Billie Jean" and the anger of "Beat It" without the grace of either. The song suggested how hostile Michael, despite his massive success, felt toward a world that judged him by standards that he rejected as beneath him.

My friends in the entertainment business at the time used to joke about people in the industry suffering from "kingitis," meaning they had been so seduced by their own success that they saw everyone around them—coworkers, lovers, family—like servants. At age thirty, Michael was king of his own domain, which didn't isolate him from criticism but did keep anyone who didn't do what he said at arm's length. Or just outside the gates of Neverland.

THE THIRD AND
FINAL FATHER

M ICHAEL WAS RAISED IN WHAT WAS IN SOME ways a very traditional family, with Joe a real old-school patriarch and his mother a quietly solid center. Yet in his professional life, Michael had a slew of surrogate parents, many of them celebrities or behind-the-scenes forces who offered tangible, hands-on help (Berry Gordy, Paul McCartney); gave him advice on stardom (Diana Ross, Elizabeth Taylor); or inspired him (Charlie Chaplin, Jackie Wilson). Michael was constantly in search of new information on the art of entertainment even as his personal life became more removed from day-to-day existence. But it is his role as father that I find so fascinating because I believe that for the last twenty or so years of his life, Michael became his own father figure.

He'd been prodded, cajoled, struck, and cultivated by his biological father, a relationship that molded Michael as a performer and scarred his sensitive psyche to a degree he never could escape. Quincy Jones, one of his mentor fathers and perhaps the most important among them, guided and facilitated Michael's growth from young man to adult artist. Michael developed to the point that he felt he'd outgrown Quincy's advice and even chafed at having to treat him as a peer.

Both Joe Jackson and Quincy Jones, products of a tough midwestern working-poor world that Michael had escaped before being completely shaped by it, had served Michael's talent and profited handsomely from it as well. (You could toss Berry Gordy into this mix as another crucial father figure if you like, but his connection to Michael seems less visceral, more distant, than Michael's bond with Joe or Quincy. Also their relationship was complicated by Jermaine's marriage to Gordy's daughter Hazel, which changed the dynamic among everyone in that circle.)

After *Bad*, his last album with Quincy, and the *Victory* tour, his last obligation to his brothers and father, Michael followed his own compass, shedding his fathers, real and surrogate, and becoming a father himself. Crucially, Michael saw himself as a father not only to his three kids, but also to all the world's children.

Intertwined with this idealized vision of himself as a benign, eternal protector of the innocent was a self-righteous rage that spilled over into much of the music he made from

1987 until 2009. For every sweet, sexy "Remember the Time," there were a number of songs that seemed aimed at his father, the media, dangerous women, or, perhaps subconsciously, himself. The ongoing theme of predatory women, from "Billie Jean" through "Dirty Diana" and others, was as insistent a trait as in the music of Jay-Z or other hip-hop artists. There's no doubt that Michael admired, even idolized, women, but any desire for them seemed tempered (or maybe blunted) by his suspicions. This father didn't need a wife to complete him, nor did he want a mother around to compete for his children's affections.

In his world he was a monarch, something apparent in his moniker as the King of Pop, his endless stream of military jackets, and the quasi-fascist iconography of his videos (such as his use of the Romanian Army as extras in the pompous concert DVD shot in Bucharest in 1992). Yet after the *Bad* album, which did well but didn't come close to matching *Thriller,* Michael knew he had to compete for record sales with younger stars, particularly in the United States, where musical memories can be short.

IT'S OFTEN BEEN OBSERVED that for athletes the legs are the first to go. They don't run as fast, jump as high, or fool others as easily with clever footwork. I think a similar thing is true of pop stars. As they age, they don't move as swiftly or as gracefully onstage, and their understanding of dance music erodes. When pop stars are young, making music, creating danceable music for peers, comes easily, because they are their own audience as much as fans are. Ray Charles, James Brown, Stevie Wonder, Prince, and Michael Jackson, men who made some of the greatest jams of their era, found their commercial fortunes begin to ebb as soon as they lost touch with the dance floor.

Their musical skills don't erode, however. In fact, with age and wisdom, musicians are capable of ever more sophisticated, emotional performances. Charles had many poignant late-career ballads, and Stevie Wonder and Prince, well past their commercial prime, are still capable of solid mid-tempo records. Ballads, which require a sense of drama and real musical acumen to execute well, can be performed ably at every age. But to consistently fill a dance floor with young people is a rare gift for a recording artist older than thirty and almost impossible for singers who are past forty.

So sometime between *Bad* in 1987 and *Dangerous* in 1991, Michael made a fateful decision. He'd been working with Quincy Jones as his primary producer for ten years, from age nineteen to twenty-nine, which in pop music terms is almost three lifetimes. In the twenty-first century, one producer rarely does one whole album with an artist, much less three. On the face of it, Michael chose Teddy Riley as his new muse, but in truth he replaced Quincy with himself. Even though Teddy would produce most of *Dangerous* and contribute to much of Michael's recorded output, over the course of his final albums Michael worked with a wide range of producer/writers, often in search of dance floor credibility and contemporary sounds.

FOR MICHAEL, and all progressive pop artists of the last forty years, there were two dance-based movements you had to come to terms with. The first was disco, which Michael easily absorbed into his DNA because disco was really an extension of the danceable R&B music he'd already been making. The second force was hip-hop, which was based primarily on the beats and, to a lesser degree, on the hooky choruses of the R&B that Michael had been reared on. And compared to a great many of his peers, he utilized the rhythmic energy of hip-hop well—at least for a while.

I interviewed Teddy Riley in 2007 when VH1's *Hip Hop Honors* celebrated his fusion of hip-hop and R&B. Our interview eventually drifted into a long conversation about his working relationship with Michael Jackson, which revealed the singer's working methods and eccentricities in the post-Quincy era. "Michael had originally reached out to me for the *Bad* album, but there was a mix-up and it didn't happen," Teddy recalled.

When I spoke to Michael, we kinda talked like we were cousins already, like family, 'cause he was like, "You're going out to California." I said, "I am?" He said, "Yes. I already got your plane ticket." So he had the ticket and everything for me to come the following Tuesday. This was a Friday. I flew to California from Virginia, where I was building my studio. So the plane trip took five hours, and from LAX they took me to the helicopter dock, which flew me to Neverland.

When he landed, Teddy saw lots of animals and security.

They were coming out of the ground. You know like they just appeared. First thing they did, they had me sign this contract agreement, saying that anything you see here on Neverland, you must never talk about. So I signed it and they took me into the house to this room with everything in it. He had this chess set. It was actually platinum and gold. I went to touch this piece. He was right behind me and he taps my shoulder.

We laughed and then we went to another room and we sat down and he started asking me all the things I liked. He just started asking me everything about my life and how I came up with songs. His favorite song of mine was "We Can Spend the Night" by GUY. He said, "I love this song. I want a song like this." Then we went from that room to the game room, which had pretty much everything you could imagine. He showed me that and then took me to his zoo. We just kind [of] chopped it up from there.

After the Neverland tour and the getting-to-know-each-other pleasantries, Michael got down to specifics, asking

Teddy what studio he liked to use in LA. Riley favored Larrabee, so Michael made a deal with the studio to create bedrooms for both men because, in Michael's words, "we're gonna be there a long time." The singer told Riley he envisioned them working on the album for as long as a year. In fact, Riley would work with Michael on the *Dangerous* album for fifteen months after their initial meeting.

The budget for such a commitment at a major LA studio in the 1990s was at least $1 million. And a lot of that time was definitely wasted. If you want to get an idea of how Michael got into financial trouble, listen to this:

> We were working on vocals and in the middle of the session, Michael Jackson left out. I thought he was going to take care of some business in the city. He actually left out and took a plane to Australia. I didn't know what to do. He called me from the plane and said, "Teddy, I had to take a very important trip." I said, "I thought you were coming back to do vocals." Michael was headed Down Under to appear at the opening of a new mall he owned and wouldn't be back for a week or two.

This attitude was so different from that of the disciplined young artist of the early 1980s who came to work focused and cut *Thriller* in roughly seven months. While Teddy was working in LA, other hot black pop producers, from L. A. Reid and Babyface Edmonds to "Jimmy Jam" Harris and Terry Lewis to Dallas Austin, would be cutting songs intended for

Michael. At the time of his death, there were hundreds of songs—some completed tracks, some half done, some just demos—in Michael's archives with everyone from Akron to Will.i.am. (Several tracks on Justin Timberlake's *Off the Wall*–flavored *Justified* were originally written for Michael by the Neptunes, such as the song "Take It from Here.")

None of these other working relationships seemed quite as intensive as Riley's, however. Over fifteen months, Riley got quite homesick for friends and family on the East Coast, but Michael wouldn't give him permission to leave LA. "I told him, 'Man, I miss my family. I miss my friends. I miss my dog.' Michael just said, 'Bring everybody to California.'" So Riley's other producing partners, many friends, his kids, and a couple of cousins were all relocated to California on Michael's dime for an open-ended visit. "It was just so crazy how that whole project went," Riley recalled with a laugh.

Though haunted by Michael's need for control and waste of money, some of Michael's best post-*Thriller* music came out of his collaboration with Riley. The most compelling composition was "Remember the Time," the closest thing in quality and feel to a classic such as "Rock with You." The song was one of thirteen tracks that Riley brought with him to LA for Jackson, but its final form was dictated by the singer's approach to songwriting. Riley, a product of the drum machine era, worked from the rhythm track out:

[My style is] going bang out the beat, get the vocals and write on the spot. Or write it and come back in two hours.

His method is leave all the tracks, leave all the keyboards, and we're going to this room with a piano. We're gonna do this old style. . . . So thank god for the skills that I have abilities to actually play a little. I started playing some things for him and he started singing and I started playing what he was singing. I started playing the chords to "Remember the Time" and he said, "I like that"; he started doing the beat box and we came up with the song.

I asked him what was the next move. He said, "Go make the track." But the track was already done, so I kinda played a trick on him. I already had it prepared. I like my music loud and he likes his louder than loud. So he brought in Emmanuel [Lewis] in the room and said, "Man, you gotta check this out. I'm telling you it's hot." I was really in suspense because Michael said, "Start the track over." So we finally start the track and Emmanuel Lewis is up there doing the electric boogie and poppin' and everybody is like "We got to finish this. We got to get it out there." We did this the first or second month I'm out there. The album didn't come out until nine months later.

In Michael's post-*Thriller* world, deadlines meant nothing, having hot tracks meant nothing. He would work on music until he was satisfied or, finally, forced to finish it.

We're working on this album and nothing is really pushing Michael to get this album out there until Tommy Mottola and the company started putting out commercials. They already had their timeline. Now he's already skipped maybe one, two, three release dates. So I was at the hotel and he woke me up with a call. "Teddy, you got to get over here right now. I need your help on this. And then you have to go back to Virginia to mix this." So I went back to VA to mix the song "Dangerous" 'cause he liked the sound of my place in Virginia.

Teddy would end up adding percussion and some other elements to "Black or White" as Michael finally rushed to complete the long overdue project. "He always asked me, 'You think we're finished with this song?' and I always said, 'Yeah, we're finished.'"

The other seminal Jackson-Riley collaboration was "Jam," and not because the video featured the world's two greatest MJ's—Michael Jackson and Michael Jordan. Whereas new jack swing defined 1990s R&B, "Jam" would establish a template for the future. Back when Rod Temperton first began writing for Michael, he noticed the singer's extraordinary facility for singing short, percussive notes. So Temperton focused on creating melodies that incorporated staccato rhythms. With "Jam," Michael, Teddy, and their studiomates took this tendency to the next level.

On the verses Michael spews words across the track like an AK-47 assault rifle, a ferociously controlled vocal that is as close to rapping as a singer can come. The glib-tongued Heavy D, a longtime Riley collaborator, rhymes on the bridge with his typical deep-voiced grace, but he is no match for Michael's clipped, emotionally charged cadences. This rapid, chopped-up approach to melody would be picked up by a new generation of artists and songwriters, children of both Michael and hip-hop. Hit-driven urban radio in the twenty-first century is filled with songs written with quarter notes and eighth notes and can sound constricted to ears used to longer melody lines.

But in the hands of R. Kelly ("Ignition") or Beyoncé Knowles ("Bills, Bills, Bills," "Single Ladies [Put a Ring on It]"), these notes sound like what they are: a clever singer's response to the rhythmic power of MCs. In fact, the ubiquity of the short-note cadence has allowed many MCs to sing/rap to access melody in their material. From Ja Rule to 50 Cent to Lil Wayne, most of the most commercially successful figures in twenty-first-century hip-hop have applied their limited vocal ability, but heightened rhythmic sense, to songs structured this way.

MICHAEL'S RELATIONSHIP TO hip-hop is actually surprisingly intimate. All of his post-Quincy producers mention Michael's use of the beat box. Whether from listening to Doug E. Fresh or Biz Markie or the Fat Boys, Michael became enamored with the use of his voice to create beats and suggest rhythm arrangements. He'd use the beat box to explain the feel and pace he wanted for a track to the younger musicians he was now working with, many of whom had been toddlers when *Thriller* was first released. Around the

Internet, tapes of Michael beat-boxing can be found, all reflecting his dynamic rhythmic sensibility. Sadly, I haven't yet heard a tape of Michael actually rhyming MC style, but he must have given it a try at least once.

Michael's recordings, both with the Jackson 5 and his solo records, have been a rich source of hip-hop samples. Naughty by Nature's "O.P.P" took the teenybopper innocence of "ABC" and transformed it into an upbeat anthem of infidelity in 1991. SWV, a new jill swing female vocal trio, made excellent use of Michael's "Human Nature," weaving his voice through a cutesy pop song of their own. Rap icon Nas used the same song as the foundation of his "It Ain't Hard to Tell" from his classic *Illmatic* album. De La Soul and Tupac Shakur are just a couple of other major hip-hop artists to make significant use of Michael's music. However, Michael most obviously influenced Usher (who sang movingly at the Staples Center tribute) and Justin Timberlake, both performers who consciously pay homage to Michael in their stage moves and many of their recordings.

Michael's impact on female performers of this generation is just as strong. Just as Michael was a legendary workaholic, Beyoncé has made her own mark as a relentless perfectionist with a taste for onstage drama. I used to work out at a posh Upper West Side athletic club. One afternoon when I was there to play some basketball, I noticed a very determined young light-skinned black woman grinding away on the Stairmaster, with a trainer and rather large man hovering nearby. On closer (but not too close) inspection, I saw that the woman with the do-rag, sweat-soaked athletic tee, and plastic workout pants was Beyoncé, then an emerging star on the verge of something bigger. I don't know how long she'd been climbing that particular mechanical mountain, but she was still on it long after I'd played my third two-on-two game in a row.

Later that week, Beyoncé made a spectacular appearance at the MTV Video Music Awards at Radio City Music Hall. Dangling from the high ceiling with a thick rope wrapped around one of her legs, Beyoncé then descended to the famous stage and immediately moved into some show-stopping choreography. As I sat in my seat, I knew I was witnessing a defining moment for this young artist. It wasn't the moonwalk on *Motown 25,* but it was an exciting performance for a music channel that hadn't yet completely capitulated to the reality TV monster.

It's funny to me that Beyoncé's hard work, which is apparent in her singing, performance style, and tour schedule (not to mention athletic workouts), is one of the chief criticisms leveled at her. Her workaholic tendencies have made many unfairly label her as robotic or mechanical. The recording techniques of contemporary dance pop, which is Beyoncé's sweet spot, are all about brittle, digital timbers, tight chromatic melodies, and sounds not found in nature. I must admit her signature chopped-up verses, which encourage a kind of rap singing, can sound more strenuous than sensuous. All of which makes you feel her music doesn't soothe, but it does engage.

With Michael as a role model, the lady is clearly consumed with some form of pop world domination. In my travels to places such as India and Brazil in the last few years, I've seen that Beyoncé is one of the few relatively young African American recording artists with a high profile. That happens only with a consistent flow of material and a willingness to travel overseas to support the music—both of which this Houston native has been diligent about.

In contrast to the gifted neo-soul generation that preceded her (Lauryn Hill, D'Angelo, Erykah Badu, Maxwell), folks who made smashing debuts and then got sidetracked by eccentricity and self-doubt, Beyoncé has put her head down and done the work. That she's managed by her father, Matthew Knowles, and left a successful group, Destiny's Child, to go solo make the MJ parallels even stronger.

But Beyoncé's narrative seems remarkably unmarred by personal demons. She has been able to appear in several commercially successful motion pictures, she has her own clothing line, and she has married a man who's as confident as she is, which by contemporary show biz standards is as normal as it gets. However, the chances of any Beyoncé album having a *Thriller*-sized success are slim, to say the least, because she's a star in the wrong era of pop music.

IF YOU WANT TO KNOW how much the record industry has contracted, just look at my Facebook friends: ex-head of Urban Music at EMI; former record promotion executive at Epic; former program director at a major R&B station, now working in digital media for an ad agency; vice president for publicity at RCA, now selling real estate. And the list goes on. These folks took me to lunch, hosted listening parties, and flashed their corporate Am Ex cards with pride. A lot of them got pushed out by hip-hop in the 1990s, which was a major generational upheaval in the industry, but a lot of them would still have jobs at major labels if those companies had not become dinosaurs.

These were definitely self-inflicted wounds. I was teaching a course at New York University in, of all things, the history of the record industry in 2001 when the school's entire e-mail system crashed. Several other universities had the same experience. The crashes were caused by something called Napster, which, being a veteran record biz insider, I had no idea even existed. My NYU students, who were participating in a pilot program for a record industry major funded by mogul Clive Davis, schooled me in the intricacies of file sharing. The future was here: peer-to-peer music with no payments, no royalties, no copyright protections.

The Recording Industry Association of America, the umbrella organization representing the legal and lobbying interest of the major labels, came up with the silliest counterstrategy of all time: Let's sue the kid who designed the technology—young Shawn Fanning—and the thousands sharing free music. Even though Napster would eventually be neutered, file sharing stayed virile. This punitive stance by the industry leaders alienated consumers, musicians, and media alike and did nothing to stem the technological tide.

In fact, it just reinforced the record industry's unsavory (and often earned) rep as a bastion of greedy scoundrels. Moreover, the industry did little to develop its own online music sales capabilities, clinging to a brick-mortar-business model that made money selling the containers (vinyl, CDs, cassettes) as much as the music inside. The industry fell behind the tech curve in the beginning of this century and remains there to this day.

Power has shifted from the corporate labels to scattered fiefdoms, decentralized around stars (Jay-Z, U2, Green Day), tastemaker sites (Pitchfork Media, AllHipHop.com), hardware manufacturers (Apple), and various nonmusic corporate underwriters. The days when Walter Yentikoff at Sony (or Mo Ostin at Warner Bros. or Clive Davis at Arista) could funnel an artist, such as Michael Jackson, Prince, or Whitney Houston, through pop radio, national record chains, and MTV to ensure maximum attention seem as ancient as a Motorola high fidelity stereo. This is not to say these old tools aren't still employed (see the Jonas Brothers, Miley Cyrus), but now audiences receive and use media in ways that make the old top-down model just one cog in a multispoked wheel. The corrupt simplicity of the old record business has been replaced by the chaotic democracy of today.

Stars still emerge from music, but they are dwarfed by *Guitar Hero, Grand Theft Auto,* and the rest, video games in which music is an important piece, but the game itself is the star and a much bigger business. In fact, music is an aspect of every leisure-time activity in video games or is central to so many sites on the web. But it is no simple thing to galvanize a planet around a singer. It happened only rarely before Michael Jackson and hasn't happened since his peak. What are the chances of it happening again? Not much.

SEARCHING FOR TRANSCENDENCE

THE NARRATIVE OF SUCCESS IN AMERICA EQUATES financial achievement with virtue. We like to imagine that artistic greatness reflects and, in some instances, projects our grandiose national identity. Even the long record of drug addicts, alcoholics, and suicidal artists in our national creative canon hasn't totally punctured our desire to idealize our artistic heroes. Even funnier is that we act surprised and often outraged when these artists turn out to be flawed human beings—just like us. Nevertheless, it can be hard to reconcile great art with personal behavior some would characterize as despicable, disreputable, or just plain crazy.

I eventually came to terms with this dichotomy by acknowledging that great art is a projection of an individual's highest, most evolved self and that its creation flows from the God within them, an inner energy that transcends their everyday human traits. The transcendent power of art derives directly from how it connects the creator and the audience to the highest, most divine part of themselves. It pulls us out of the dirt, clutter, and frustration of our day, connecting us to the best parts of our souls.

All of which brings me to the artistic impact of the sex scandals that started in 1993 and that dogged Michael until his death. I don't know what transpired between Michael and Jordon "Jordy" Chandler, whose father, Evan, accused the entertainer of molesting his son and set off investigations and revelations about Michael's personal life that continued on well after those initial charges were dismissed.

Chandler, then a Beverly Hills dentist, would forever change Michael's public image (much more so in the United States than overseas) and cast a sinister shadow on his eccentricities past (Bubbles the chimp, the Elephant Man's bones) and future (his brief marriages to Priscilla Presley and Debbie Rows, covering his children's heads with blankets and veils in public). When Michael went on international television and advocated sharing his bed with little boys who weren't his children, the audience saw clearly how isolated and delusional he'd become. No one living in the real world would have been all right with such an admission. The effect of the pedophile accusations, and of his own public statements, on his art was profound. From 1979 to 1991, he'd released four full-length albums. From 1993 to 2009, he released only two albums of original music and one remix album. Between 2002 and 2009, he released no new music. Between the domestic backlash, arguments with his record label, and his own indulgent production process (and lifestyle), a man once so consumed with work stopped doing what he had been born to do.

That anger in his voice, an element of his vocal approach that had been evolving for years, appeared in much of the tracks on *HIStory* and *Invincible,* but for so many years he was mute, but not unproductive. He built hospitals in poor countries and gave millions to charities. He lived for a time in the Middle East and was befriended by a sheikh who became a business partner. He raised three kids and was viewed by all who came in contact with his family as a doting, dedicated father.

He did make music—and lots of it. John Barnes, an extraordinary keyboardist and one of Michael's longtime, closest musical associates, was working on cataloging Michael's vast archive of unreleased recordings even before his death, much of it made since 2000. So at some point in the next few years, expect a torrent of Michael Jackson music, a flood that could dwarf the many hours of posthumous Tupac Shakur rhymes and the endless repacking of Elvis Presley's performances. In that mass of music, you can bet there will be a gem or two that were left buried while Michael spent most of his focus on his precarious finances and gradually became a slave to debilitating medications.

Nevertheless, that yearning for transcendence, that quality he possessed and that possessed us, was what he communicated for his fifty years on earth. He did it as a child with an adult's instincts, as a gifted teenage apprentice, and as a master craftsman. The problem every pop star faces in the rock era is that the music business is a young person's game. It's even more of a challenge when by your midtwenties you've already conquered that world. The adult Michael Jackson never quite found what he was looking for, but at least he left us enough music, both familiar and not yet known, so that we can continue his search ourselves.

THIS IS IT

O
N OCTOBER 28, 2009, I, LIKE THOUSANDS around the world, bought a ticket to see *This Is It,* the 111-minute documentary carved out of an estimated 110 hours of rehearsal footage shot for Jackson's personal archives. Despite the international hype and folks dressed up at midnight shows around the globe, I walked up to the box office at the Cineplex theater on Third Avenue and East 11th Street with my friend Tigist Selam, and I purchased two tickets for a mostly empty 1:45 p.m. show. Inside the basement theater we watched the film with about ten other Jackson fans.

Sony released the film in some 8,000 theaters worldwide, with an additional 3,000 in the United States. That's a nice number of domestic theaters for a documentary about an unfinished concert. But international enthusiasm appeared much higher for the film, with even China, not a place usually considered a safe harbor for valuable U.S. copyrights, booking the film so that it opened concurrently with screenings here.

Although our theater wasn't crowded, the online chatter about *This Is It* was standing room only. Reviewers across the globe weighed in and, sometimes reluctantly, found merit in the documentary. "'This Is It' isn't Michael Jackson at his greatest; it's him preparing to be his greatest. But watching that preparation is gift enough," wrote Tom Long of the *Detroit News*. "There's no sign of sickness here, no sense of an artist past his prime. Instead you see a performer at his peak," wrote a surprised Stephen Whitty of the *Newark Star-Ledger*. CNN's Tom Charity didn't want to recommend the film but finally admitted, "Yes, you probably want to see this." On the Rotten Tomatoes ratings of reviews from the nation's top film critics, the film received an outstanding 86 percent rating, a real tribute to the smart work director Kenny Ortega (of *High School Musical* fame) and his team of four editors did.

On Twitter and Facebook, fans were mostly ecstatic. But in the online space, there was a large, well-organized minority who saw *This Is It* as a collage of lies. "On June 25, 2009 Michael Jackson died. He was 50 years old and the father of three young children. Were you shocked? You should have been," wrote the folks at a web site titled "This Is Not It." "In fact, the true state of Michael Jackson's failing health was being hidden from you by those who are making a profit from the screening of the 'This Is It' movie." Furthermore, the site stated, "a few scenes were selected in which Michael Jackson smiled and showed that in spite of being in a dire state, he was still the greatest star in the world."

Having been in scores of edit rooms over the last ten years, I know "This Is Not It" is likely more right than wrong. Any edit of 110 hours of footage into under 2 hours of film could yield dozens of different versions. Moreover, any version of the documentary financed by the promoters of the London shows was unlikely to include any images that suggested Jackson was near death's door during rehearsals. The popular narrative was that the preparation for these shows killed the superstar. As I sat in my seat, I was sure no visual evidence of that theory would be on the screen.

My friend Tigist, an actress-writer of Ethiopian/German descent, a woman who was introduced to Jackson's work as a child by *Thriller* while living overseas, teared up the first time Jackson appeared on screen. In fact, for most of the movie's running time, she was either crying or red-eyed, saddened all over again by the singer's death.

AT FIFTY, MICHAEL IS a tall, imposing man, with huge hands and long arms. He is clearly underweight, and even though the film doesn't make him look sickly, he definitely looks frail. There are no close-ups of Jackson in the film. We never get closer than a shot from the waist up, and mostly we see him at middle distance, an adoring remove from our gaze, far enough away for us to see his grace but never close enough for us to be truly intimate with him. His face—the skin, the nose, the eyes—almost feels hidden in plain sight.

This visual strategy makes clear something quite extraordinary. Michael is actually a better, more complex dancer than earlier in his life. Compared to his cocky, committed team of dancers, Michael isn't as athletic or explosive. But the precision of his movement, how he glides from stage left to right, his sharp head and body turns are more glorious than ever. He appears to hear several kinds of rhythm: the beat of Jonathan Moffett's trap drums, the bass lines played by Alex Al, and then internal eight counts where he interjects combinations of hand gestures, shoulder shakes, and dance steps.

Watching Michael move recalls listening to a skilled drum circle, where a master drummer creates the central rhythm and other percussionists circle his beat, sometimes joining the central pattern and other times floating off to construct a new rhythm that the other drummers may follow. Jackson dances like that master drummer. It is his feel for "time," both for rhythm and the pauses between beats, that guides him through the rehearsal.

Phrases such as "Let it breathe" and "I'll feel it" pepper his instructions to his collaborators. In conversations with director Kenny Ortega and musical director Michael Bearden, Jackson is very precise about what emotion a song, a piano part, or a lighting cue can create when properly placed, all of which are elements of timing. Joy, pain, and pathos are all conjured by what he'd call "magic," but what I'd call a unique sense of space and time.

Jackson is careful throughout the rehearsal footage with his vocal chords. Sometimes he sings all the words to a song. Often he leaves out parts of verses, especially on up-tempo numbers when he's focused more on dance moves or staging. This isn't unusual for a performer in rehearsal, but when you see the rigor of the planned show and Jackson not having done a full-on series of concerts in half a decade, you have to wonder how he'd have gotten through fifty concerts. My plan had been to attend one of the first ten to fifteen shows in London, figuring he'd still be in good shape and in peak voice.

Two moments in the film, one troubling and the other sublime, lingered with me well after I left the theater. During the Jackson 5 medley, Jackson looks uncomfortable. At one point, he stops singing and complains about the sound mix in his headphones, saying his ears feel punched by the sound. The amateur Freud in me suspects the real source of his discomfort is singing those long-ago songs associated with his ten-year-old self, that round-faced, bushy-haired dynamo from Gary, Indiana.

But maybe that's me projecting my own discomfort onto the singer. The truth is that watching him perform those songs of his (our) youth pulled me right out of the movie, sending me back to Madison Square Garden, watching him gyrate, all brown and 1970s fly. Until he does "I'll Be There," I accepted this tall, pale figure as Michael Jackson. When he sings, "Just look over your shoulder honey," I heard that child's voice from the Motown records and felt alienated from this man because those Jackson 5 songs are so connected to a particular "Black is beautiful" period. That pictures of the prepubescent Michael Jackson accompany the songs only heightened my disconnect from the film.

And yet this Michael Jackson or, at least, the latest incarnation of the man is a person fully invested with the DNA and talent of that long-gone little brown boy. His "Billie Jean" at *Motown 25* back in 1984 was the defining moment of Jackson's career. Several generations have moonwalked in his wake. However, his "Billie Jean" performance in *This Is It* is, I think, a bit of perfection that confirms his legacy.

Within the "Billie Jean" dance, which is as familiar as any of Jackson's catalog, Jackson reinvents himself on the Staples stage. Using his arms and fingers and holding his torso at precise angles that dramatize every movement, Jackson remakes "Billie Jean" as a dance for an older, wiser man. His dancers go crazy (though they'd gone crazy at other times, too), but here their cheers are indeed warranted. And at the end of this magnificent dance, Jackson says, "Well, we got a good feel for it." No one watching this dance will shrug it off so casually, just as no one watching will understand how dope that performance is more than its dancer. Yet at the time Jackson did this dance, it was simply some sweet moves at a rehearsal and nothing more. But now, and forever, it is Michael's last act of magic.

EPILOGUE

I T IS THE NIGHT AFTER MICHAEL JACKSON'S DEATH, and I am in a Clinton Hill, Brooklyn, nightspot named Spudnik, with sweat dripping down my face as DJ Spinna rocks a creative remix of "ABC." A beautiful, bootylicious young woman named Maya, with her belly ring showing and a determined scowl on her face, dances close enough to kiss me. The look on her face isn't one of anger, but of joyous intensity. She is riding the beat hard—just like the five hundred or so people jam-packed on this basement dance floor.

I have come to Spudnik with a group of friends, all of us united in the desire to celebrate Michael Jackson's life by hearing his voice and music bang through large, well-modulated speakers. All day long has felt like 1984, with *Thriller* on the way to becoming the biggest album of all time. From the booming systems of passing cars, from the iPods of people on the subway, and from the outdoor speakers of a DJ at a basketball tournament, Michael's voice fills the air in Brooklyn like streaks of sunshine on this cloudy Saturday. Out in Los Angeles, Michael's body is undergoing an autopsy to determine why this fifty-year-old man went into cardiac arrest. Here in Brooklyn, and all over the world, people are buying and listening to the mountain of recordings he left behind.

I am drenched in sweat. So is everyone around me. Drops of condensation begin to drip from the ceiling. I turn my head toward the sky as the heroic intro to "Can You Feel It" fills the room. And I can. RIP Michael Jackson.

ACKNOWLEDGMENTS

Thanks to Robert Christgau, Mark Rowland, Adam White, Radcliffe Joe, Von Alexander, John McClain, Steven Ivory, Ed Eckstine, Teddy Riley, John and Stephen Barnes, the late Earl Van Dyck, and Quincy Jones for the conversations and help over the years that informed this narrative.

INDEX

Aarons, Richard, 47
"ABC," 36, 198, 215
Acoustic Recording Process,
    81
Aerosmith, 123
Africa
    "black" Americans and,
        87–92
    Jackson 5 and, 90–92
    music concerts, 88–89
Ailey, Alvin, 107
"Ain't Nobody Here but Us
    Chickens," 113
"Ain't That Just Like a
    Woman," 114
Al, Alex, 212
Ali, Muhammad, 48, 88
"All Along the Watchtower,"
    117

All-State TV commercials, 38
"All That I Got is You," 39
Allen, Richard, 153
Alvin and the Chipmunks, 43
"Always and Forever," 96
AM Chicago, 165
Amadeus (movie), 157
Amsterdam News weekly, 50
Anderson Tapes, The, 71
"Another Part of Me," 182
AOR (album-oriented rock),
    117, 118
Apollo Theater, New York,
    21
Ashford, Jack, 32
ATV Music catalog
    Beatles and, 106
    Michael Jackson and, 106
Austin, Patti, 136

Awake magazine, 17

Azoff, Irving, 159

"Baby, Come to Me," 136

"Baby Be Mine," 95, 99

"Baby It's You," 101

Back on the Block, 137

"Bad"/*Bad*, 138, 178, 179, 180–181, 185

Bad tour, 181–184

Badham, John, 54

Bahler, Tom, 63

Ballard, Glen, 183

"Bambi," 122

Bar-Kays, 53

Barnes, John, 207

Beach Boys, 117

Bearden, Michael, 212

Beat box, 197–198

"Beat It"/video

about/making, 119–122, 124, 156

emotions and, 83, 84

Peters and, 108–109

public service announcement, 167

Beatles

antitax strategy/effects, 105–106

ATV Music catalog, 106

black music and, 101, 117

popularity, 145

See also specific individuals; specific music

Beatty, Talley, 107

Becker, Walter, 130

Bee Gees, 54

Bell, Thom, 39

"Ben," 62

Benatar, Pat, 109

Bennett, Michael, 108

Benson, George, 80

Berry, Chuck, 115–116, 117, 123

"Best of My Love," 97

BET awards, 25

Bettis, John, 131–132

Betty Davis, 118

Beverly Center, Los Angeles, 77–78

Beverly Hills Cop (movie), 165

Beyoncé, 27, 197, 198–200

"Big Boy," 28

Big Daddy Kane, 177

Billboard magazine, 113, 120

covering Michael Jackson, 66, 146–150, 151–152, 154–156, 157, 158–160, 169, 170–171

"Billie Jean"/video
about/making, 59, 125,
126–128, 138, 151, 156,
189
awards, 165
credits, 81
emotions and, 83–84, 126
This Is It, 214
"Bills, Bills, Bills," 197
Bishop, Joey, 47–48
"Black Cat," 122–123
"Black English," 148
Black music
Beatles and, 101
children imitating adults,
28–29
corporate takeover, 23
See also specific groups;
specific individuals;
specific types
"Black or White," 196
Black Rock Coalition, 123
Blackmon, Larry, 150–151
"Blame It on the Boogie,"
58
Blaxploitation movies, 68
Bobo, Willie, 88
Bodyguard, The, soundtrack,
55
Bono, Sonny, 47, 48

Booker T. and the MGs, 71,
133
Born to Run (Marsh), 156
"Boys," 101
*Boyz n the Hoo*d (movie), 20
Braithwaite, Freddy, 7
Braithwaite, Kwame, 91
Branca, John, 69
"Breakin' Away," 152
Brown, 139
Brown, Eddie "Bongo," 32
Brown, James, 29, 30, 41, 60,
88, 190
Brown, Jim, 70
"Bubblegum," 33
"Bubblegum soul" hits, 36
Bubbles the chimp, 206
Burke, Alohe, 20
Burke, Betty, 20
Burke, Clarence, 20
Burke, Clarence Junior, 20
Burke, Dennis, 20
Burke, James, 20
Burke, Kenneth (Keni), 20
Bush, George W., 166
Butler, Jerry, 30

Cable news, 8–9
"Caldonia," 113
Caldwell, Hank, 153

Cameo, 53, 71, 122, 150
"Can You Feel It"/video, 60–61, 62, 216
"Candy," 122
Carlos and Charlie's, 70
Carpenter, Karen, 63
Carpenters, 132
Chancler, Ndugu, 80–81, 126–127
Chandler, Jordan/Evan, 206
Chaplin, Charlie, 187
Charity, Tom, 210
Charles, Ray, 31, 32, 63, 134, 190
Chi-Lites, 30
Chicago, 131
Chong, Tommy, 29
Chorus Line, A, 108
Christian, Charlie, 114
Christmas Carol, A (Dickens), 108
Chuck D, 177
Citizen Kane, 9
Clan, 34
Clayton, Merry, 118
CNN, 25, 210
Cobain, Kurt, 27
Cohen, Marty, 47
"Cold Sweat," 30

Color Purple, The (Walker), 149
Comin' Uptown, 108
Commodores, 3, 97, 98, 134
Con Funk Shun, 53, 71
Controversy, 122
Conway, Tim, 47–48
Cornelius, Don, 43, 68
Corporation productions, 36, 37
Corse, Katherine. See Jackson, Katherine Corse
Cosby, Bill, 24, 43
Cosby, Hank, 34
Cosby Show, The (TV), 71, 165, 176
Crack epidemic, 177
"Crazy for You," 132
Crocker, Frankie "Hollywood," 52–53, 59, 89
Crouch, Andraé, 183
Crow, Sheryl, 184
Cruz, Cecila, 88
"Cult of Personality," 123

Dangerous, 190, 193
"Dangerous," 196
Darling, Cary, 151

Davis, Clive, 201
Davis, Hal, 37, 38
Davis, Miles, 132
Dawn of the Dead (movie), 109
De La Soul, 198
De Passe, Suzanne, 41
"Dead Giveaway," 122
Dean, Debbie, 33
DeBarge, El, 137
Deke and the Deacons, 33
Del Barrio, Eddie, 97
Delfonics, 39
Dells, 101
Deluise, Dom, 47–48
Destiny, 58, 62
Details magazine, 185
Detroit News, 210
Dibango, Manu, 89, 92, 93
Dickens, Charles, 108
Diddley, Bo, 115
Digital recording technology, 80
"Dirty Diana," 124, 189
Dirty Mind, 122
Disco, 50–55, 89, 98, 149, 191
"Do the Fonz," 47
Do the Right Thing, 7

"Does Your Mama Know About Me?" 30
Domino, Fats, 115
"Don't Leave Me This Way," 97
"Don't Look Any Further," 182
"Don't Stop the Music," 93
"Don't Stop 'til You Get Enough"/video, 59, 61–62
Dozier, Lamont, 34
Dr. Buzzard's Original Savannah Band, 53
Dramatics, 57
Dreamgirls, 108
Dude, The, 131–132, 133, 134, 135, 152
Dylan, Bob, 53

Earth, Wind and Fire, 68, 71, 97, 98, 118, 127
"Easy," 97, 134
Ebony, 42
"Ebony and Ivory," 102, 103, 104
Ed Sullivan Show, 12, 43, 46
Edmonds, Kenny, 68
Edwards, Dennis, 182

"Elvis Is Dead," 123–124
"Enjoy Yourself," 58
Epstein, Brian, 105
ESPN, 10
E.T.: The Extra-Terrestrial
    (movie), 154
ET children's album, 165

Fagen, Donald, 130
Falana, Lola, 108
Falcons, 18–19
Fall Out Boy, 124
Fania All-Stars, 88
Fanning, Shawn, 201
"Fantasy," 97
Fat Albert (TV), 43
"Five Guys Named Moe," 113
Five Stairsteps, 20
Flack, Roberta, 88
Fonda, Jane, 51
"Fool for You, A," 32
Foreman, George, 88
Four Seasons, 101
Four Tops, 32
Foxx, Redd, 48
"Foxy Lady," 117
Franklin, Aretha, 108
Friday Night Videos (TV), 59
Fullfillingness' First Finale,
    103

Funk Brothers, 31
Funkadelic-Parliament,
    98–99, 117–118

Gabler, Milt, 114
Gamble, Kenny, 58, 97
Gap Band, 68, 71
Garcia, Byron F., 110
Garrett, Siedah, 182–183
Gary, Indiana
    in 1960s, 15–16
    in 1970s/1980s, 22
    black empowerment, 15–16
    racism, 16
    Steelton Records, 27–28,
        29, 33
    white flight, 16
Gaye, Marvin, 28, 30, 68, 98,
    134
General Hospital (TV), 136
"Georgy Porgy," 131
Ghostface Killah, 39
Gibb brothers, 54
Gilbert, Cary, 97
"Gimme Shelter," 118
"Girl Is Mine, The," 76, 102,
    104–105, 154
"Girlfriend," 72, 102,
    103–104
Give Me the Night, 80

Gladys Knight and the Pips, 35

"Glamour Boys," 123

"Goin' Back to Indiana," 36–37

Goin' Back to Indiana (TV special), 46

Goldberg, Whoopi, 165

Gordinier, Jeff, 185

Gordy, Berry
  Jackson 5/Michael and, 32–33, 41–42, 43, 187, 188
  Richards and, 33–34, 35
  writing by, 35, 36, 38
  See also Motown

Gordy, Hazel, 188

Gore, Leslie, 79

Goree Island, 90, 91

"Got to Get You into My Life," 118

"Gotta Serve Somebody," 53

Grade, Lord Lew, 105

Grateful Dead, 117

Great Hall, Toronto tribute, 139–140

Grein, Paul, 170–171

Grier, Pam, 68

"Groove Line, The," 95

Grosvenor, Vertamae, 168

Grunge, 110

Guest, Anthony Haden, 50

Guinness Book of World Records, 7, 164

Guns and Roses, 123, 124

Haley, Bill, 114

Hansberry, Lorraine, 18

Harris, Eddie, 88

Hatcher, Richard, 15–16

Hathaway, Donny, 45

"Heartbreak Hotel," 33, 64, 83

Heatwave, 95–96

Heavy D, 196–197

Hendrix, James Marshall "Jimi," 116–117, 118, 123, 124, 155

Hey, Jerry, 127

"Hey Joe," 117

High School Musical, 210

Hilburn, Robert, 155, 170

Hip-hop, 32, 110, 176, 177, 191, 197, 198, 201

Hip Hop Honors, 12

Hirshey, Geri, 156

HIStory, 207

Hogan, Carl, 113, 114, 115

Holland, Brian, 34

Holland, Eddie, 34

Holland-Dozier-Holland, 102
Hook (movie), 154
Hooker, John Lee, 101
Hooks, Robert, 90
Hopkins, Jerry, 156
Houston, Whitney, 55, 135, 153, 168
"How Do You Keep the Music Playing," 135–136
Howling at the Moon (Yetnikoff), 145–146
Huff, Leon, 58, 97
Hughes, John, 110
"Human Nature"
  about, 38, 129–130, 131–132, 156, 198
  credits, 80–81
Hungate, David, 130
Hutch, Willie, 37, 38

"I Can't Help It," 104
"I Got the Feeling," 30
"I Just Can't Stop Loving You," 182, 184
"I Want to Be Free," 35
"I Want You Back," 33, 35, 36–37
Ice T, 177
"Ignition," 197

"I'll Be There," 38, 39, 63, 213
Illmatic, 198
ImageNation, 90
"In the Navy," 110
Ingram, James, 133–138
Innervisions, 103
Introducing … the Beatles, 101
Invincible, 207
Ironside (TV), 71
Isley, Ernie, 118
Isley, Ronnie, 28
Isley Brothers, 32, 101, 118
"It Ain't Hard to Tell," 198
"It Was a Very Good Year," 45–46
"It's Real," 137
"It's Your Thing," 32

Jabara, Paul, 97, 99
Jackson, Chuck, 3
Jackson, Freddie, 137
Jackson, Jackie (Sigmond Esco)
  Africa and, 91
  childhood, 17, 19, 68
Jackson, Janet
  career, 65, 122–123, 124, 137

Gary, Indiana, 17
Jackson family (TV) series, 46, 47
Jackson, Jermaine
    childhood, 17, 68
    interviews, 57, 168–169
    Jackson 5, 29, 32, 38, 39
    solo career, 58
    Victory tour and, 158, 168–169
    wives, 158, 188
Jackson, Joseph
    background/childhood, 18
    CNN appearance after son's death, 25
    daughters' careers and, 65
    description, 65–66
    Jackson family (TV) series, 46–47
    music playing/bands, 18–19
    personality, 25, 65
    Victory tour and, 158, 159, 169–170
    wedding, 16–17
    work of, 18, 19
Jackson, Joseph/as parent
    black working-class context, 24, 25, 187
    descriptions of, 20–21, 22–23, 25

Jackson 5, 21, 22, 45
    Michael's will and, 66
    Michael's work ethic and, 21
    racial context and, 24–25
    scenario without Joseph's push, 22–24
Jackson, Katherine Corse
    background, 17
    Jackson family (TV) series, 46
    as parent, 17, 187
    Victory tour and, 158, 159, 169–170
    wedding, 16–17
Jackson, LaToya
    career, 65, 137
    childhood, 17
    Jackson family (TV) series, 46, 47
    marriage, 65
Jackson, Marlon
    childhood, 17, 68
    Jackson 5 and, 58
Jackson, Maureen (Reebee), 17
Jackson, Michael
    anger, 83–84, 185, 188–189, 207
    charities and, 207

Jackson, Michael (*continued*)
  death/aftermath, 7, 9,
    215–216
  eccentricities, 206
  as father, 187, 188–189, 207
  father-figures of, 187–188
  films and, 44–45
  financial problems, 9, 193,
    194, 207
  fire/Pepsi commercial, 162,
    163, 166
  glittering socks, 59, 61, 184
  Grammy awards (1984),
    165, 166
  on Grammy nominations/
    Off the Wall, 99
  military jackets, 158, 167,
    189
  minimovies of/by, 45
  nose job, 162, 168
  painkillers, 162, 207
  relationship with father, 66,
    188
  sex scandals, 115, 206
  sibling relationships, 62
  singing voice, 45
  skin/cosmetic changes, 12,
    44, 162, 163, 168,
    180–181, 184–185
  speaking voice, 44–45

unreleased recordings, 194,
    207
  views of himself, 45, 185,
    188–189
  will of, 66, 69
Jackson, Michael/childhood
  Africa and, 91–92
  Gary, Indiana, 17
  Jackson family (TV) series,
    46, 47, 48
  Jehovah's Witnesses and,
    17, 18
  in Los Angeles, 68–69
  performance style, 46
  relationship with father,
    25–26, 188
  scenario without father's
    push, 23–24
  voice and, 68
  youth vs. poise, 45–46
  See also Jackson 5/Michael
    Jackson
Jackson, Randy (Steven
    Randell)
  childhood, 17
  Jackson 5 and, 58, 61, 62
  Jackson family (TV) series,
    46
  song writing, 58, 62
Jackson, Reverend Jesse, 167

Jackson, Tito (Toriano Adoyl)
    childhood, 17, 19, 68
    Jackson 5 and, 58, 64
    Jackson family (TV) series,
        47
    musical beginnings, 19
Jackson 5
    Africa, 90–92
    beginnings of, 19–20
    cartoon series (TV), 43–44
    clothes/hair, 42
    Davis and, 37, 38
    groupies, 125
    image, 41–44
    Jermaine Jackson, 29, 32,
        38, 39
    Joseph Jackson, 21, 22, 45
    Madison Square Garden
        (1971), 1–3
    Marlon Jackson, 58
    medley in *This Is It*,
        213–214
    Motown beginnings/Taylor,
        29, 30–32, 33, 36
    "music video," 41
    Randy Jackson, 58, 61, 62
    records, 35–37, 38–39
    variety shows, 43, 46
    *See also specific individuals;
        specific songs*

Jackson 5 in Africa, The
    (film), 90–91
Jackson 5/Michael Jackson
    lessons learned, 37
    mimicking older singers, 28,
        29, 30, 33, 41, 45–46
    songwriting, 58
    soul-singing, 31
    vocal approach and, 37
    voice and, 27, 31, 33, 38,
        62–63
    See also specific songs
Jackson family (TV) series,
    46–48
Jagged Little Pill, 183
Jagger, Mick, 123
"Jam," 196–197
Jam, Jimmy, 69
James, Rick, 57, 70
Jarreau, Al, 152
Jehovah's Witnesses
    about, 17–18
    "Can You Feel It" video
        and, 60–61
    Jackson family and, 17, 18
    Michael's music and, 60–61,
        84
Jet, 42, 168
Jheri curls, 12, 58
Johnson, Howard, 150

Johnson, Louis, 127
Jones, Quincy
  on artist-producer
    relationship, 81–82
  background, 71, 78, 79
  on digital recording, 80
  interviews, 78, 79–80,
    81–83
  on Michael, 82, 185
  music productions, 62, 71,
    103, 104, 119, 120–121,
    126–127, 128, 131–132,
    138, 140–141, 165, 182,
    183
  personality/description,
    79–80, 136
  Qwest label, 135–136, 183
  relationship with Michael,
    72, 188, 190
  Spielberg and, 149, 154
  on Temperton, 96
  Wiz, The, 49–50
  See also specific music
Jones, Uriel, 32
Jordan, Louis, 113, 114–115
Jordan, Michael, 10–11, 165
Josie and the Pussycats (TV),
  43
Journey, 131

"Jump," 121
"Jump blues," 114
Jungle Fever, 180
"Just Once," 134, 136
Justified, 194

Kaufman Astoria Studios, 50
Keith, Gordon, 27
Kelly, R., 197
King, B.B., 88, 116
King, Don, 159, 169, 170,
  171, 172
King, Evelyn, 150
Knack, 119
Knowles, Matthew, 200
KRS-One, 177
Ku Klux Klan, 16

"Lady in My Life," 139–141
Landee, Donn, 121
Landis, John, 107
"Last Dance," 97
Last Party, The (Guest), 50
"Leave Me Alone," 47, 185
Led Zeppelin, 53
Lee, Spike, 7, 8, 93
Leiber, Jerry, 96
Leiviska-Wild, Nancy, 151
Lennon, John, 101, 102, 103

Leviticus, 53
Lewis, Emmanuel, 195
Lewis, Jerry Lee, 115
Lewis, Terry, 69
"Liberian Girl," 12, 182
Limp Bizkit, 123
Lincoln Center Library,
    Manhattan, 147
Little Miss Soul, 30
Living Colour, 118, 123–124
Long, Tom, 210
Los Angeles
    about, 67–68, 70
    Motown and, 37, 65, 67–68,
    70
Los Angeles Times, 155, 170
"Love Child," 34
"Love Hangover," 37–38
"Love Is a Battlefield," 109
"Love to Love You Baby," 53,
    108, 149
"Love You Save, The," 36
"Lovely One," 62
"Lowdown," 97
Lukather, Steve, 119–120,
    130, 131, 132
Lumet, Sidney, 72
Lymon, Frankie, 21, 35
Lynn, Cheryl, 131

Madison Square Garden
    concerts
    Bad (1988), 183–184
    Jackson 5 (1971), 1–3
    Jacksons (1981), 57–59, 61
Madonna, 123, 132, 184
Main Course, 54
Makeba, Miriam, 88
Maldonado, Margaret, 158
"Mama's Pearl," 36–37
"Man in the Mirror," 183
Man with the Horn, The, 132
Mancuso, David, 89
Manhattans, 135
Mann, Barry, 134
Mardin, Arif, 54
Markeljevic, Ines, 111
Marsh, Dave, 156
Martin, George, 104
Mason, Vernon, 179
Massenburg, George, 127
"Maybe Tomorrow," 39
Mayer, John, 129–130, 132
Mayfield, Curtis, 20, 45, 98
McCann, Les, 88
McCartney, Linda, 102, 170
McCartney, Paul
    black music and, 101, 102,
    103

McCartney, Paul (*continued*)
  Lennon and, 102, 103
  relationship/collaborations
    with Michael, 72, 76,
    103–104, 105, 154, 156,
    170, 187
  style of, 102
McClain, John
  background, 69–70, 168
  Michael's will and, 69
McDonald, Michael, 137
McKay, Al, 97
Michael Jackson Story, The
  (George), 7–8, 156–158,
  161–162, 164–165, 168
"Michelle," 103
Minnelli, Liza, 50, 126
Mizell, Fonce, 34–35
Mod Squad (TV), 71
Moffett, Jonathan, 64, 212
Moon Walk (Michael
  Jackson), 25, 140–141
Moore, Melba, 150
Morissette, Alanis, 183
Morris Day and the Time, 57
Morrison, Jim, 156
Mother's Finest, 118
Motown
  Jacksons' break from label,
    46

Los Angeles, 37, 65, 67–68,
    70
  style strategies, 36–37
  See also specific *individuals*
Motown/Jackson 5
  beginnings/Taylor, 29,
    30–32, 33, 36
  cartoon series, 43–44
  image, 41–44
Mottola, Tommy, 195–196
Mozart, Wolfgang Amadeus,
    157
MTV, 59, 78–79, 110, 120,
    123, 124, 151, 199, 202
Murphy, Eddie, 28, 44, 70,
    165
Musical segregation (1960s-
    1970s), 117–118
Musician magazine, 79, 120–
    121, 149, 175
Musicians and youth, 189–
    190, 208
"My Ding-a-Ling," 116
"My Sharona," 119

Napster, 201–202
Nas, 198
National Public Radio
  commentary, 168
Naughty by Nature, 198

"Negroes" term, 87
Neverland, 9, 177–178, 185, 192
New Edition, 36
New Jack City (movie), 180
New Kids on the Block, 36
New York
  disco era, 50–55
  Michael Jackson/*The Wiz* filming, 49, 50–52, 53, 55
New York Times, 8, 156, 164, 179
Newark Star-Ledger, 210
"Nights on Broadway," 54
Nike commercial, 106
1984 (Orwell), 161
No One Here Gets Out Alive (Hopkins and Sugerman), 156
Northern Songs, 105
"Not My Lover," 125
  See also "Billie Jean"

"O-o-h Child," 20
Obama, Barack, 24, 166
Off the Wall
  description, 59, 61–62, 63, 64, 83, 95, 150, 155–156
  Grammy nominations and, 99
  production, 71, 72, 82, 103, 150
  success, 60, 99, 150, 155–156
  See also specific songs
"Off the Wall," 62
O'Jays, 97
Onassis, Jacqueline Kennedy, 25
"One Hundred Ways," 134
O'Neal, Tatum, 126
"O.P.P.," 198
Ortega, Kenny, 210, 212
Orwell, George, 161
Osmonds, 36

Paich, David, 97, 130, 131
Paradise Garage, 53
Parks, Dean, 81
Parliament-Funkadelic, 98–99, 117–118
Patterson, Vincent, 109
Peaches and Herb, 135
Pepsi, 159, 170
Pepsi commercial/fire, 162, 163, 166
Perrin, Freddie, 34–35
Perrine, Valerie, 51
Perry, Edmund shooting
  about, 178–179
  Bad and, 179, 180–181

Perry, Jonah, 178, 179
Peters, Michael
  background, 107–108
  Michael Jackson and,
    108–109, 112
Phillinganes, Greg, 127
Phillips, McKenzie, 47
Pickett, Wilson, 18–19, 116
Pointer Sisters, 132, 171
Poitier, Sidney, 44, 71
Poncia, Vini, 97
Porcaro, Jeff, 81, 130
Porcaro, Steve, 130, 131,
    132
Presley, Elvis, 33, 115, 145,
    155, 207
Presley, Priscilla, 206
Prince
  about, 70, 118, 122, 123,
    124
  Michael Jackson rivalry,
    155, 181
  pseudonyms, 155
  success, 57, 153, 176, 190
Pryor, Richard, 44
Public Enemy, 123, 147
"Purple Haze," 117
Purple Rain, 122
"Purple Rain," 122

"PYT (Pretty Young Thing),"
    136–137, 138

Qwest label and Quincy
    Jones, 135–136, 183

R&B
  Grammy Awards (late
    1970s), 97–99
  white songwriters, 96–99
Racism
  Ku Klux Klan, 16
  movies, 87–88
  pre-civil rights movement,
    24–25
Rage Against the Machine,
    123
Raisin in the Sun, A
    (Hansberry), 18
Rakim, 177
Rap music, 57, 137, 198
Raw concert film, 28
Ray, Ola, 111, 140
"Reach Out I'll Be There," 32
Reagan, Nancy, 166–167
Reagan, Ronald, 110, 161,
    166–167
Record industry contraction,
    200–203

Record World magazine, 57, 148

Recording Industry Association of America, 201

Regal Theater, Chicago, 21

Reid, Antonio, 68

Reid, Vernon, 123

"Remember the Time"/video, 12, 189, 194

Resane, Wenjiel, 111

"Reunited," 135

Revelation Funk, 134

"Revolution," 106

Revolution, 123

Richards, Deke
  background, 33–34
  Gordy and, 33–34, 35
  Jackson 5 and, 34–35

Richie, Lionel, 3, 97, 98, 129, 134–135, 137, 153, 170

Right On! magazine, 1, 42, 168

Rihanna, 93

Riley, Teddy, 137, 190, 191–196

Ritz, David, 30

Robinson, Fatima, 11–12

Robinson, Smokey, 33, 68, 129, 170

Robinson, Zuri, 12–13

"Rock Around the Clock," 114

"Rock with You"/video
  description, 32, 59–60, 61, 62, 64, 95
  success, 138

Rockwell, John, 67

Rolling Stone, 58, 156, 169

Rolling Stones, 118, 123

Romero, George A., 109

Roots miniseries, 71, 78

Roscoe's Chicken and Waffles, Los Angeles, 70

Ross, Diana, 37–38, 50, 108, 126, 152, 170, 187

Roth, David Lee, 120

Rows, Debbie, 206

Rubell, Steve, 51

Rubin, Rick, 123

Ruffin, David, 182

"Rumble in the Jungle," 88

Run-D.M.C., 123, 124, 165

Rural Still Life, 130

Rust Belt towns
  description, 15
  See also Gary, Indiana

Rza, 39

"Sail On," 134

Samuels, Jim, 47
Samuels and Cohen comedy team, 47
Sanford and Son (TV), 71
Santana, 88
Santilli, Ivana, 139–140
Saturday Night Fever movie/soundtrack, 54–55
Sawyer, Pam, 34
"Say Say Say," 102, 104
Sayer, Leo, 97, 99
Scaggs, Boz, 97
Scorsese, Martin, 180, 181
Scott, Shirley, 69
Scott, Tom, 128
"Scream," 124
"Secret Garden," 137
Seeka, Johnny, 90
Selam, Tigist, 209, 211
"Shake Your Body Down to the Ground," 62
Shalamar, 122
Shapiro, Peter, 52–53
She's Gotta Have It, 8
"She's Out of My Life," 38, 61, 62, 63
Shields, Brooke, 126, 164
"Shining Star," 135
Shirelles, 101

"Silly Love Songs," 102
Simmons, Russell, 57, 123
Sinatra, Frank, 46, 79, 140
"Single Ladies," 197
Slam dancing, 110
Slash, 124
Sledge, Percy, 116
"Slow Hand," 132
Smith, Larry, 123
Smokey Robinson and the Miracles, 33
"Smooth Criminal"/video, 109, 182
Snipes, Wesley, 180, 181
Songs in the Key of Life, 103
"Soul Makossa," 89, 92–93
Soul Power (documentary), 88–89, 90, 91
"Soul to Soul" concert, 88, 90
Soul Train, 42, 43, 46, 68
"Soundies" (music videos 1940s), 114
Spielberg, Steven, 44, 149, 154
Spinners, 88
Spook Show, The, 165
Sports Century, 10
Springsteen, Bruce, 156
Spudnik, Brooklyn, 215–216

Stain, 123

Staples Arena memorial, 129–130, 183, 198

Star Wars, 78

"State of Shock," 124

"Stayin' Alive," 54

Steelton Records, Gary, Indiana, 27–28, 29, 33

Steely Dan, 130

Stoller, Mike, 96

Stone, Sly, 98, 117

Street dance, 110

Stubbs, Levi, 32

Studio 54, 50–51, 52, 53

Stylistics, 39

"Sugar Daddy," 36–37

Sugerman, Danny, 156

Sullivan, Chuck, 159, 170–171

Summer, Donna, 53, 80, 97, 108, 149

Supremes, 34

Sure, Al B., 137

Sutton Place, New York, 50

Sweat, Keith, 147

Swedien, Bruce, 72, 80, 81, 127–128

SWV, 198

Sylvers, Leon, 71

Talking Book, 103

Tarzan films, 87

Tavern on the Green, New York, 158

Taylor, Bobby
background, 29–30
on Jackson 5, 30
Jackson 5/Motown and, 29, 30–32, 33, 36, 41
Jackson 5 "music video," 41

Taylor, Elizabeth, 187

Taylor, R. Dean, 34

Temperton, Rod, 95, 96, 107, 139, 140, 141, 196

Temptations, 29, 182

"They Don't Care About Us" video, 93

"Things I Do for You," 62

This Is It concert, 9, 61

This Is It documentary
description, 61, 211–214
Jackson 5 medley, 213–214
Michael's dancing, 212, 214
popularity, 209–210
reviews, 210–211

"This Place Hotel," 62, 63

"Thrill the World" dancing, 111–112

Thriller
album cover/package, 76
analog recording, 78, 80
anniversary celebration,
110
covering, 145–160
credits and, 80–81
impact/success of, 9–10, 13,
78–79, 122, 164, 165
Michael's anger/fear and,
83–84
music description, 76–77,
83–84
musical videos and, 78–79
pen-and-ink drawings, 76
recording period, 77
Westlake Studios and, 77,
78, 79
See also specific songs
"Thriller"/video
about, 107, 109, 184
Filipino prisoner video,
110–111
"Thrill the World" dancing,
111–112
Tiger Beat magazine, 42
Timberlake, Justin, 194, 198
Toto, 119, 130–131
Toto IV, 131
Townsend, Robert, 28

Travolta, John, 54
Triumph, 58, 60–61, 62
Triumph tour
about, 61–64
music videos and, 59
sound/image changes,
58–59, 62–64
Tupac Shakur, 198, 207
*Turn the Beat Around: The
Secret History of Disco*
(Shapiro), 52–53
Turner, Ike, 88, 115
Turner, Tina, 48, 88
"Twist and Shout," 101
Tyler, Steven, 51
Tympany Five, 113

"Use ta Be My Girl," 97
Usher, 129, 198

Van Halen, Eddie, 79, 119–
121
Van Houten, Lee, 178, 179
Vancouvers, 29–30
Vandross, Luther, 137
Victory Tour
announcing, 158–159
concert descriptions,
172–176
media covering, 148

problems with, 159–160, 167–168, 169–171
Video games, 202–203
Village People, 51, 110
Village Voice, 173, 174–175, 178
Vivid, 123

"Walk This Way," 123
Walker, Alice, 149
Walker, T-Bone, 115
"Wanna Be Startin' Somethin'"
 African connection, 92–94
 emotions and, 83, 84
 success, 138
Washington, Dinah, 79
Watchtower, The magazine, 17
Waters, Muddy, 102, 116
Watson, Wah Wah, 32
"Way You Make Me Feel, The," 182
WBLS radio station, 52–53, 89
"We Can Spend the Night," 192
Webb, Bruce, 152
Weil, Cynthia, 134
Welles, Orson, 9

West, Bob, 38
West Side Story, 109
Wexler, Jerry, 113
When We Were Kings (movie), 88
"When You Were Mine," 122
"Which Way to America?," 123
White, Adam, 148–149
White, Barry, 137
White, Maurice, 68, 97
White, Verdine, 97
Whitty, Stephen, 210
"Who's Lovin' You," 33
"Who's That Lady," 118
"Why Do Fools Fall in Love?" 21, 35, 152
Wilder, Johnnie, 95–96
Williams, David, 81, 119
Williams, Paul, 165
Williamson, Fred, 68
Wilson, Charlie, 68
Wilson, Frank, 34
Wilson, Jackie
 about, 28, 36
 background, 28, 60
 influence on Michael, 41, 60, 185, 187
Winfrey, Oprah, 165
Wings, 102

Withers, Bill, 88

Wiz, The, 44, 49–50, 51, 53, 55, 72

WNEW-FM radio, 118

Wonder, Stevie, 34, 68, 98, 102, 103, 129, 150, 190

"Working Day and Night," 61, 151

"Yah Mo B There," 137

"Yesterday Once More," 132

Yetnikoff, Walter, 145–146

"Y.M.C.A.," 110

Yo! MTV Raps, 7

"You Are Not Alone," 38

"You Are the Sunshine of My Life," 103

"You Make Me Feel Like Dancing," 97

"Your Body Is a Wonderland," 130

Photo by Jelena Vukotic

Nelson George is the award-winning author of a dozen books, including the classics *Hip Hop America* and *The Death of Rhythm and Blues*, and the acclaimed memoir *City Kid*. He has been a columnist for the *Village Voice* and *Billboard*, and has written for a range of magazines including *Rolling Stone*, *Playboy*, *Esquire*, and *Essence*. He is also a two-time recipient of the ASCAP-Deems Taylor Award. George was born in Brooklyn, where he still lives.